I

WEST END OF THE N

This window shows us the incident recorded in St Mark 10: 13 – 16. Jesus' followers are trying to chase away people bringing their infant children to him to be blessed, but against the prejudices of the day he shows his concern for the young and gladly takes them in his arms. A strange place to begin a grown up tour of a church's windows? Maybe not: for Jesus went on to say that no adult can ever come to know God unless they are willing to show a simple trust – a childlike faith – in him and his word. Quite a rebuke and challenge for all cynics, sceptics and the worldly-wise!

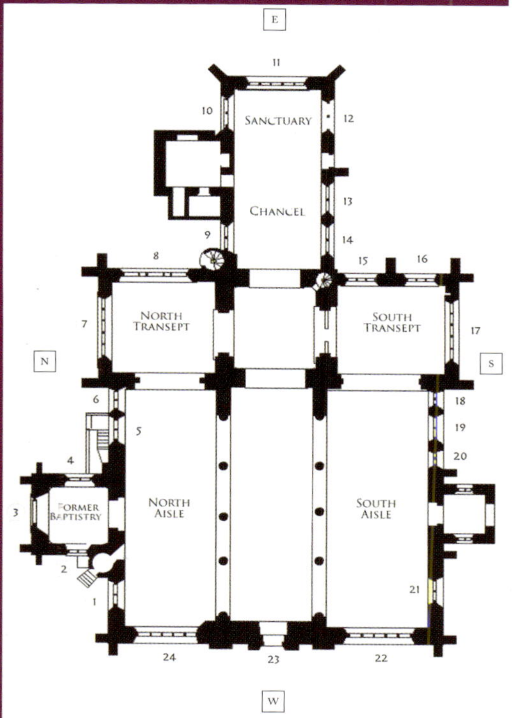

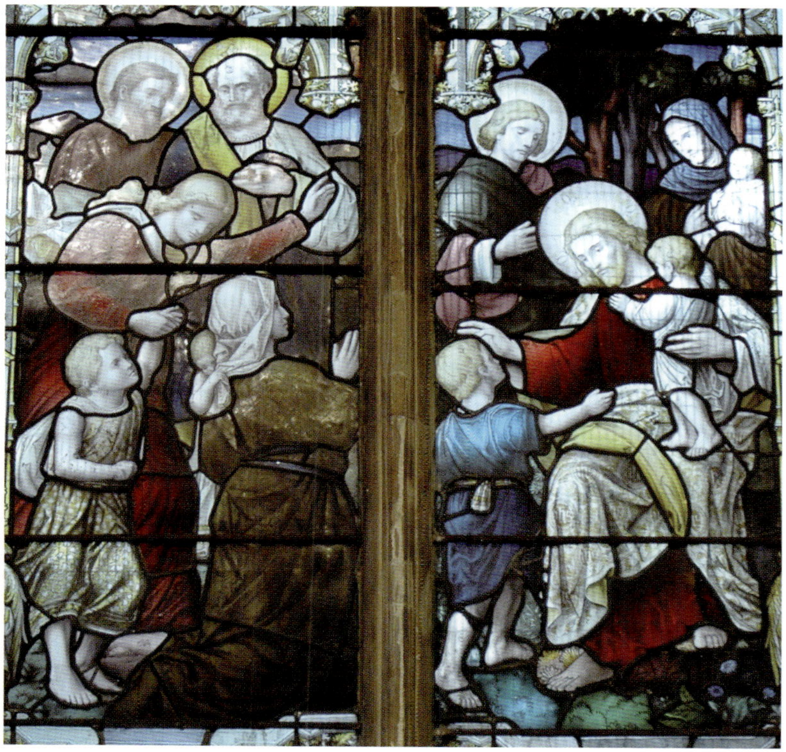

2, 3 & 4

THE BAPTISTRY (and former entrance to the church)

This fourteenth century area is the traditional place for the baptising (or christening) of infants to mark their initiation into the Church. Although the practice of baptising babies is not specifically mentioned in the Bible, there is certainly encouragement to parents to bring their newly born child into a holy place to give thanks to God for his precious gift, and to dedicate the infant to his service. So in the left hand panel of the window on the left wall we see Mary and Joseph bringing baby Jesus into the Jerusalem temple.[1] According to the Jewish law, they were supposed to bring a lamb and a pigeon for sacrifice, but Joseph is only carrying two pigeons, a concession the Law granted to the less well-off.[2] So Jesus obviously came from a poor family, and is therefore immediately identified with the world's vulnerable and underprivileged.

The right hand panel of this window shows the baby Jesus in the arms of a godly old man in the temple. This is Simeon. St Luke 2: 25 – 35 tells us that God had promised he would not die before he had seen with his own eyes the long awaited Messiah. Simeon realizes that the child in front of him is the One! He blesses the child and the parents with some memorable words.

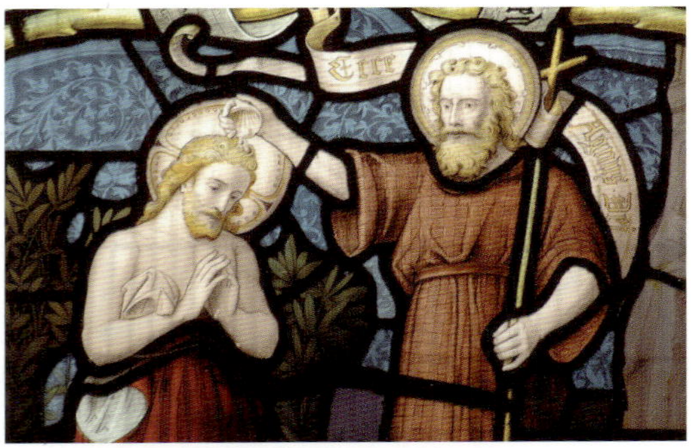

[1] St Luke 2: 22 – 24

[2] Leviticus 12: 6 – 8

[3] St Matthew 3: 13 – 17

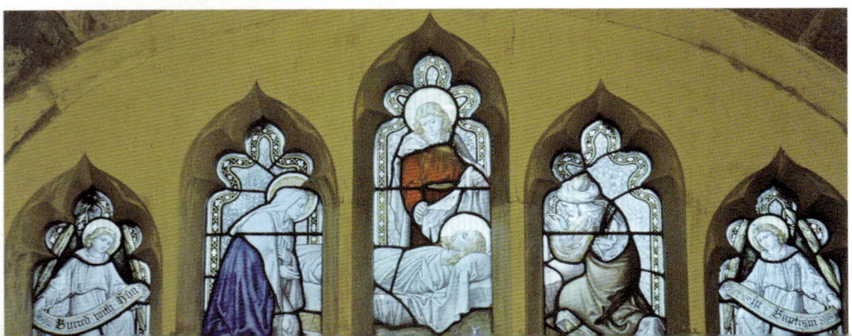

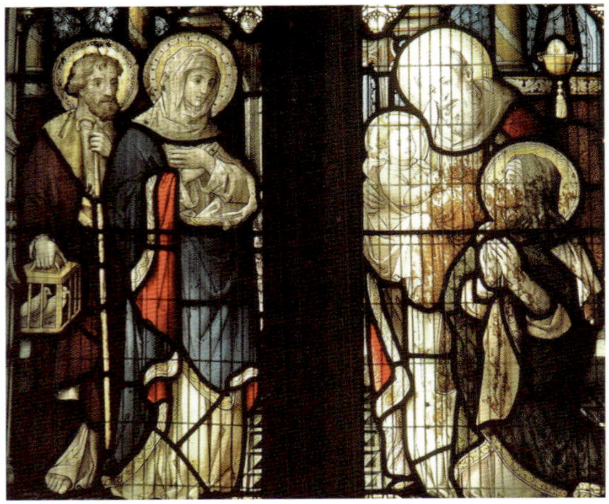

The small window straight ahead is based on a text from Romans 6: 4 - "Buried with him through baptism." When in baptism someone is immersed (or "buried") "under the water", it's as if they are sharing in Christ's own journey of death and burial, and can therefore benefit personally from his atoning sacrifice for sin. Of course Christ didn't stay buried – he rose from the dead – and in the same way the baptised don't stay under the water! They " emerge", to a new way of life where former unchristian ways are to be "dead and buried".

The window on the right hand side of the area depicts Jesus, now about thirty years old and shortly to begin his public ministry, being baptised by John the Baptist. Living a perfect life, Jesus didn't submit to baptism because he needed a personal sign of God's washing away of his own sin. Instead he saw his baptism as a way of closely identifying himself with sinful people like you and me, for whom later he would die on the cross as an atoning sacrifice.[3]

A question to consider: if you were baptised as a baby (or even later on in your life), what does it mean to you now?

5 & 6

THE NORTH AISLE

The bearded man is Moses, who received the Ten Commandments directly from God Himself, and wrote them down on stone tablets.[1] He is teaching God's people, who are listening intently. God's ten basic rules are all about what it means to love him, and to love our neighbour, and they are just as relevant today as when first compiled over three thousand years ago. Of course all of us fail with some of them, but in a way, that is part of their purpose – to reveal just how high God's standards are, and therefore how much we need his mercy and forgiveness offered through Christ.

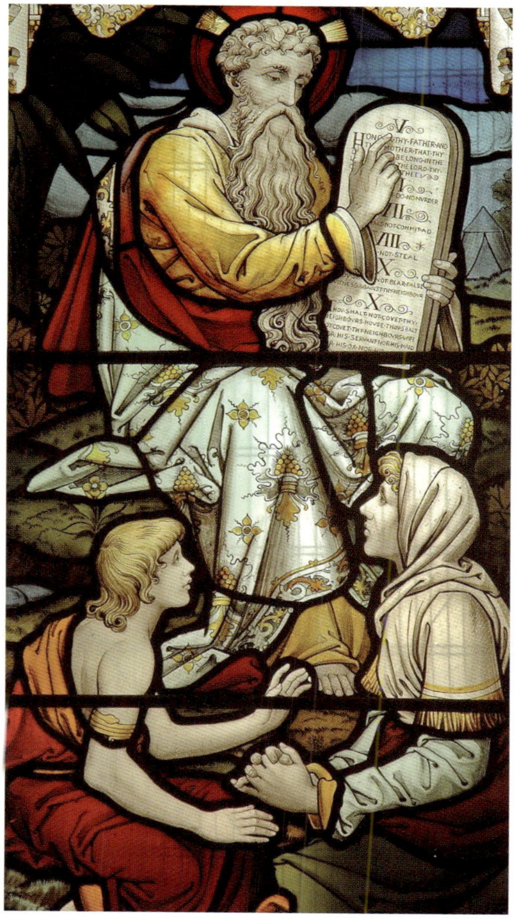

The two panels of the next window take us to St Luke 5: 1 – 11. Jesus has enabled the fishermen Peter, John, and James to haul in a miraculously big catch! They realize Jesus must be someone unique, specially sent by God. So when Jesus challenges them to give up their fishing business and become his disciples, there and then they abandon their boats and accompany him for the next three momentous years. Jesus doesn't ask us literally to abandon everything as the cost of following him, but he does demand that the whole of our lives – work, family, leisure, possessions – are yielded to his Lordship.[2]

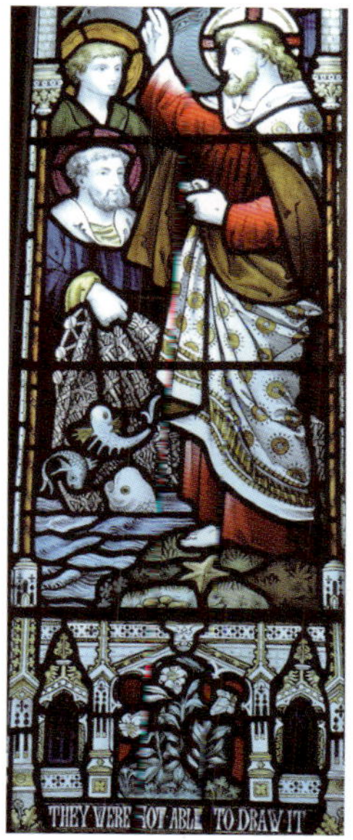

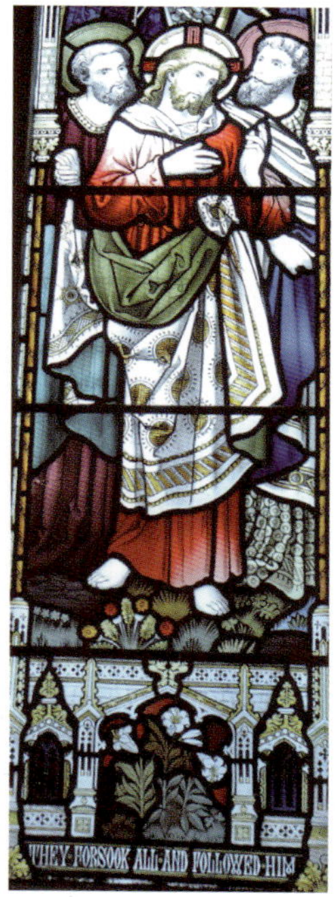

[1] Exodus 20: 1 – 17; 32: 15 – 16

[2] St Luke 9: 23 – 25

7

NORTH TRANSEPT WINDOW

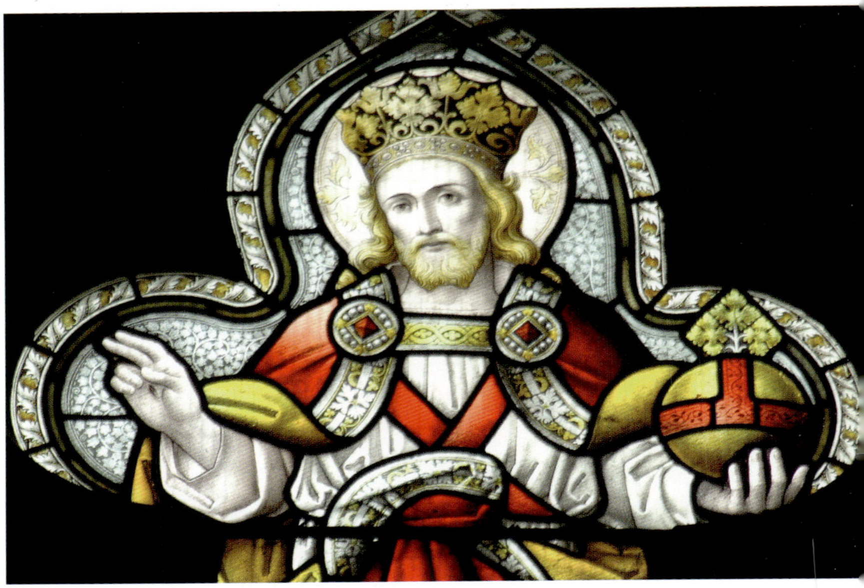

At the very top we see a representation of Jesus Christ as Lord and King, a position he has earned by his death and subsequent resurrection.[1]

The four smaller panels below depict, from left to right, Matthew, Mark, Luke, and John, the writers of the four Gospels, or biographies of Jesus.

The five larger lower windows show scenes from Jesus' life: On the far left (and slightly damaged), a story we've met before at Point 2: The godly old man, Simeon, having finally realized his life's ambition of seeing the Messiah, prays that he may soon die in peace.[2]

Second from the left, we see Jesus calling Peter the fisherman to leave his nets, and become one of his disciples (see also Point 6). Jesus tells him that he will become a "fisher of men", in other words, Peter will "catch" many people, or draw them into the Christian Faith.[3] After Jesus' resurrection, this happened – Peter preached boldly about Jesus, and many turned to Christ as a result.[4] Every Christian today is similarly called to be a "fisherman" for Jesus, not necessarily by preaching, but by the attractiveness of their lives and honest witness to what Jesus has done for them.

The middle window depicts a mysterious incident in Jesus' life, when he climbs a high mountain with his three closest friends, Peter, John and James.[5] As Jesus is praying, his face becomes as bright as the sun, and his clothes turn brilliant white.

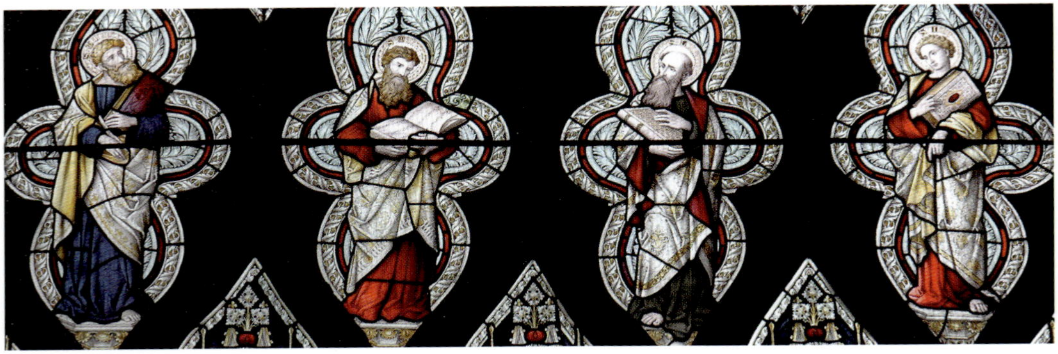

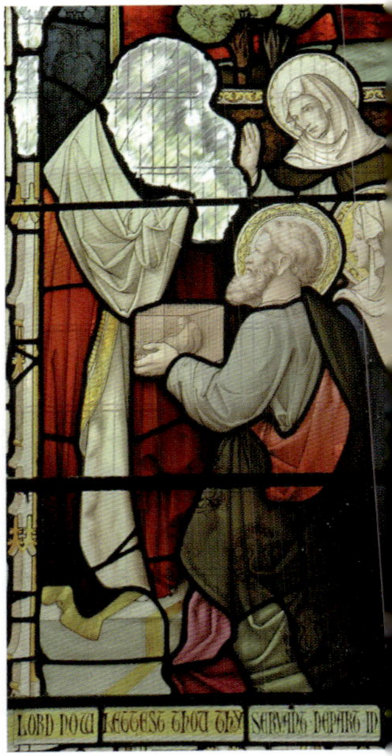

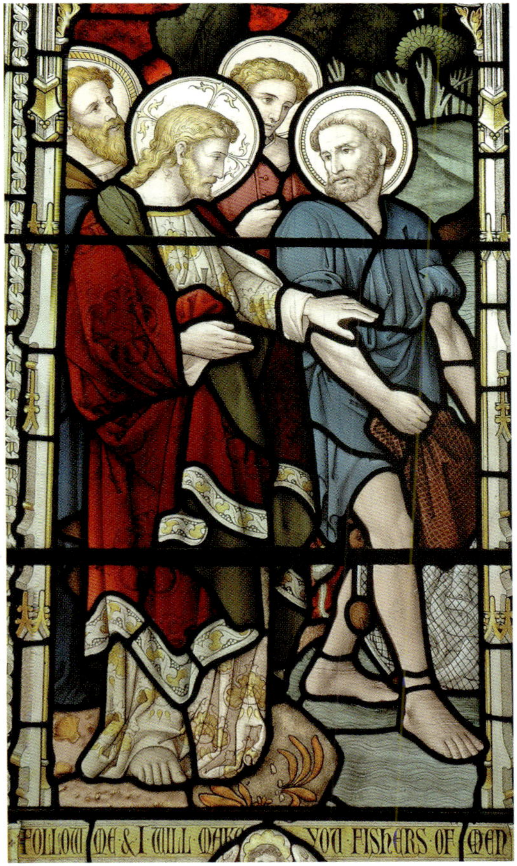

Christians call this his "transfiguration", or the brief moment when he passed from his normal earthly appearance into his heavenly state. This was to encourage Jesus before he begins his fateful journey to his cruel death in Jerusalem. Also present to encourage are Moses, shown on the left with the Ten Commandments, and the prophet Elijah (Elias) carrying the sword. These two spiritual giants from earlier centuries are reminding Jesus that his forthcoming sacrificial death was all planned long in advance by God as the only way of reconciling humans to their Creator.

The fourth window brings us to the eve of Jesus' death. He is in a garden called Gethsemane on the outskirts of Jerusalem.[6] Aware that his enemies are only minutes away from arresting him, Jesus is desperately praying for the strength and courage to see it all through. His agony is the terrible prospect of being cut off from the love of his Father God as he, the Son, carries on the cross the curse of all the sins ever committed. Notice Jesus' disciples – asleep! At his crucial hour of need, they fail him, as we often do – but his heavenly Father has sent an angel (top right) to strengthen him.[7]

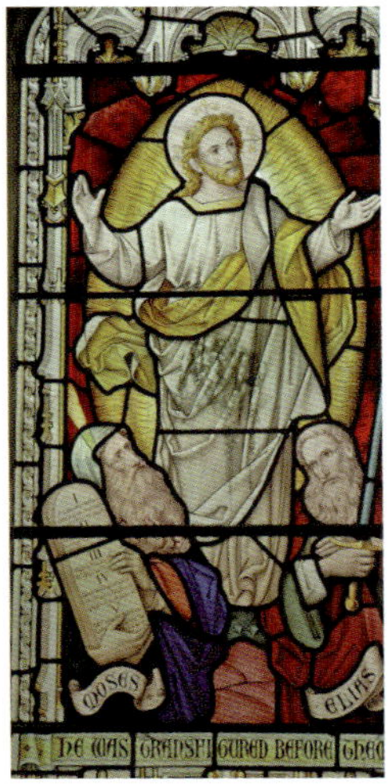

On the far right – the triumphant end of the story! This is the morning of the first Easter Day. Some of Jesus' devoted women followers have visited the tomb where he was buried, following his crucifixion on the previous Friday. They plan to embalm his body, but it isn't there – the tomb is empty! An angelic messenger explains why: "He is not here. He is risen."[8] Christianity stands or falls on the truth of this claim – that God raised his Son from the dead as proof that Jesus really is the Saviour of the world, who has conquered death and so enabled all who trust in him to enjoy "eternal life", or friendship with God into eternity.

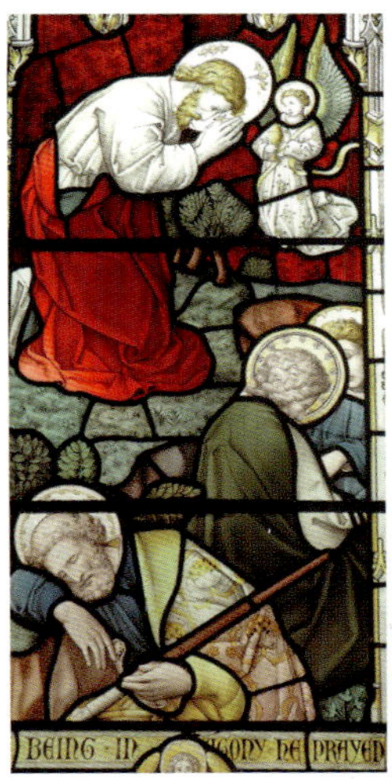

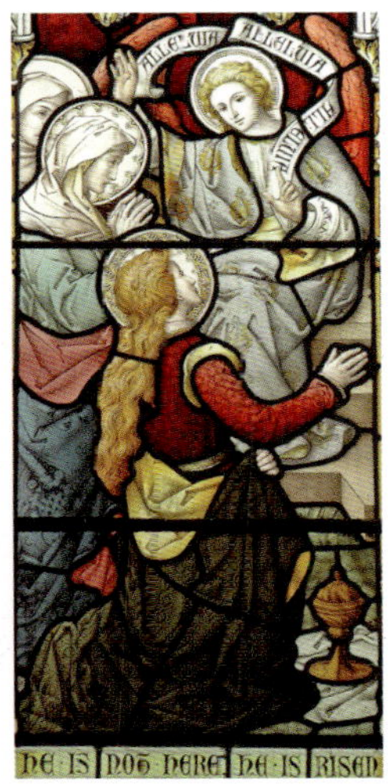

[1] Philippians 2: 8 – 11

[2] St Luke 2: 29

[3] St Luke 5: 1 – 11

[4] Acts 2: 14 – 41

[5] St Luke 9: 28 – 36

[6] St Mark 14: 32 – 36

[7] St Luke 22: 39 – 46

[8] St Mark 16: 1 - 8

8

THE ROSE, OR WHEEL, WINDOW

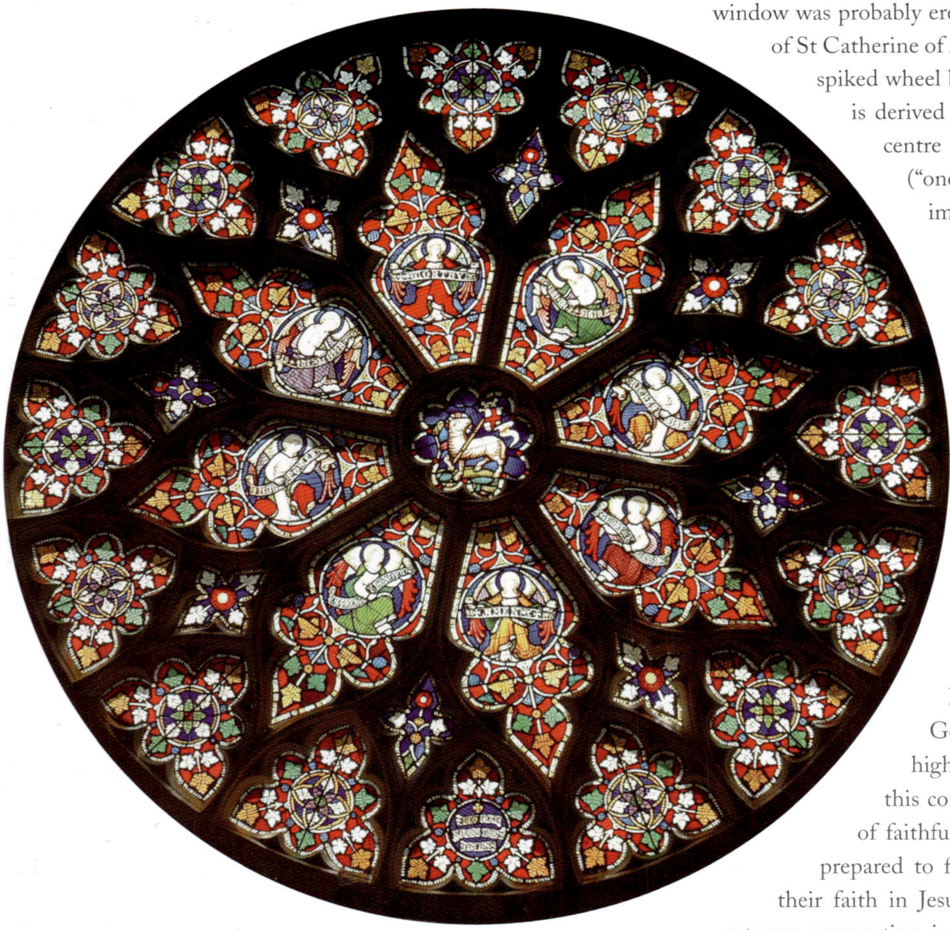

A copy of a favourite design of mediaeval craftsmen, this exquisite circular window was probably erected to commemorate the martyrdom of St Catherine of Alexandria, reputedly put to death on a spiked wheel by the Romans, and from whose name is derived the "catherine-wheel". Don't miss the centre line: It has been placed at an angle ("one o'clock to seven o'clock"), to give the impression of movement.

Right in the middle is a lamb pierced by a sword. This is the "Lamb, looking as if it had been slain" that St John describes in Revelation 5: 6. It is of course Jesus, "the Lamb of God who takes away the sin of the world" by his death on the cross.[1] Surrounding the Lamb are eight panels together displaying the text from Revelation 5:12 – "Worthy is the Lamb that was slain, to receive power, riches, and wisdom, strength and honour, glory and blessing." Because of his perfect obedience to God his Father's will, Jesus takes the highest place in the universe – and it is in this confidence that down the years, millions of faithful Christians like Catherine have been prepared to face martyrdom rather than renounce their faith in Jesus. There are Christians today facing extreme persecution in parts of the Middle East and Asia. We shouldn't be surprised at this: Jesus told his followers to expect it.[2] St Catherine and her fellow martyrs present us with this challenge: Is our love for Jesus Christ so strong that we would be prepared to pay the ultimate price of remaining loyal to him?

[1] St John 1: 29

[2] St John 15: 18 - 20

9

THE CHANCEL (North Side)

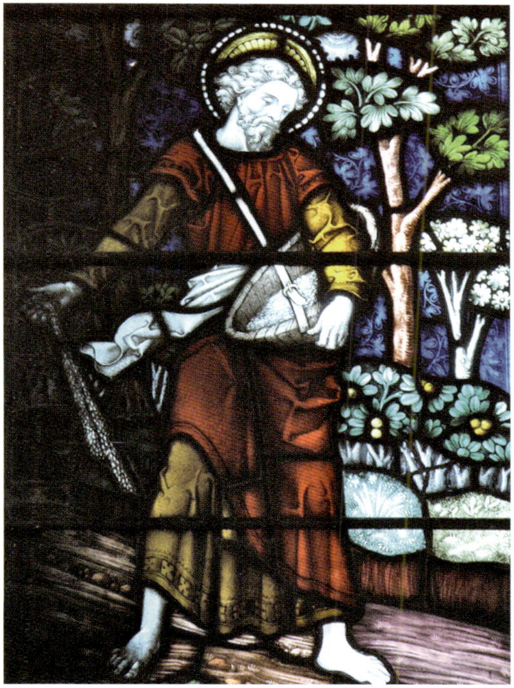

Jesus once told a story about a farmer who went out to sow his seed.[1] Some of the seed was eaten by birds, some fell into thin soil and any growth was soon scorched, and some produced a crop which was then strangled by weeds. So many setbacks for the farmer – but some of the seed fell into good soil and produced a bumper crop, making his work worthwhile. Like many of Jesus' stories, this is a parable, that is, it has a hidden spiritual meaning: The sower is God (or his representatives) and the seed is the Christian message. And the different types of soil? Well, that's us – and our response, or lack of it, to God's word! Jesus goes on to explain all this to his friends.[2]

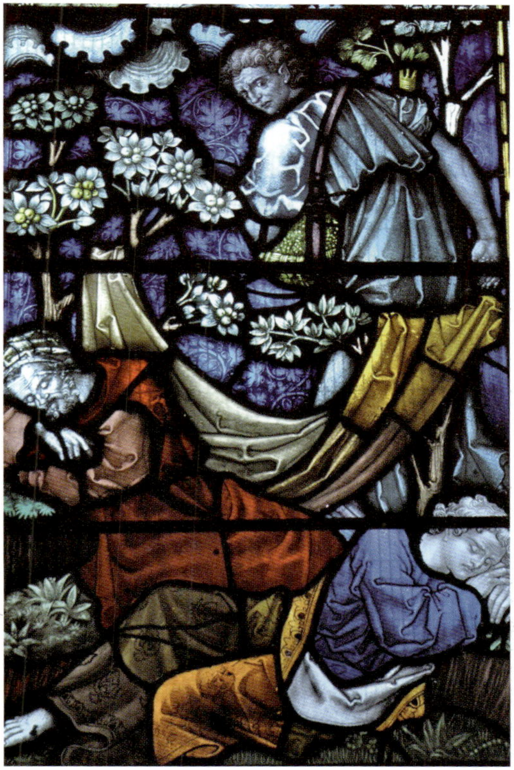

The second panel illustrates St Matthew 13: 24 – 30, 36 – 43. The sower has sown good seed, but during the night an enemy sows weeds in the same field. The result is a very mixed crop! The enemy is the Devil, or Satan, an evil force taken very seriously in the Bible, who is out to spoil God's harvest and damage the Christian Church. Jesus tells this story as a warning: this malevolent foe will always see to it that outwardly the Christian Church is a mixture of the good and the bad, the genuine "crop" and interloping hypocrites. However, God will sort it all out in the end – glance up to the top of the window, where an angel is reaping a good harvest and destroying the weeds. When Judgement Day finally comes, God will separate out the genuine from the false. The challenge for us: Which are we? Wheat or weeds, and where will we end up? In the barn, or the burner?

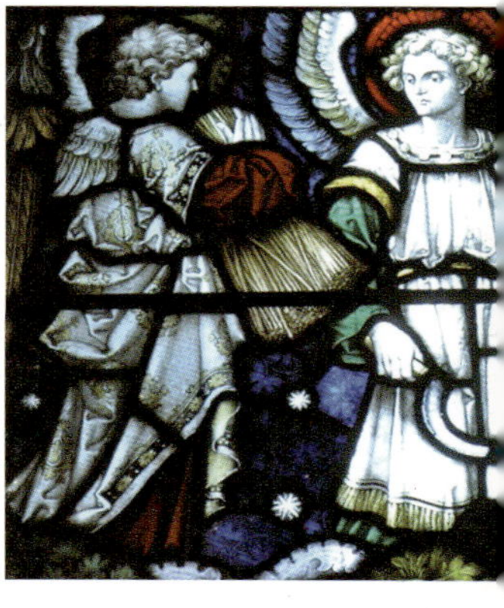

[1] St Matthew 13: 1 - 8

[2] St Matthew 13: 18 - 23

IO

THE SANCTUARY (North Side)

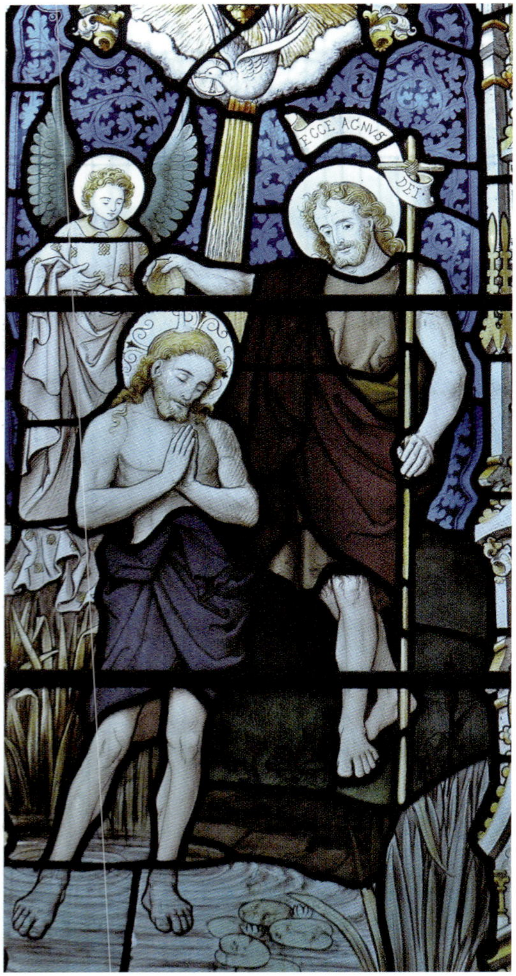

In the left hand window, we revisit the baptism of Jesus by John the Baptist (Point 4). It was John who pointed out Jesus to the crowds, saying: "Behold, the Lamb of God", or in Latin: "Ecce Agnus Dei."[1]

The dove descending upon Jesus was a sign of the gift of God's Holy Spirit coming to him, to strengthen and equip him for his ministry ahead.[2] To carry out God's will, every Christian needs the indwelling presence of God's Spirit, and He will come to us from the moment we put our trust in Jesus as our Saviour and Lord. The water of baptism is intended to be a powerful sign of the drenching of the Spirit, flooding our lives with love for Jesus Christ.

The six stone water jars in the bottom left hand corner of the second window take us straight to St John 2: 1 – 11. Jesus is a guest at a wedding feast. The supply of wine has run out, a social disaster for the hosts. The picture depicts Jesus' mother, Mary, begging him to do something! Using

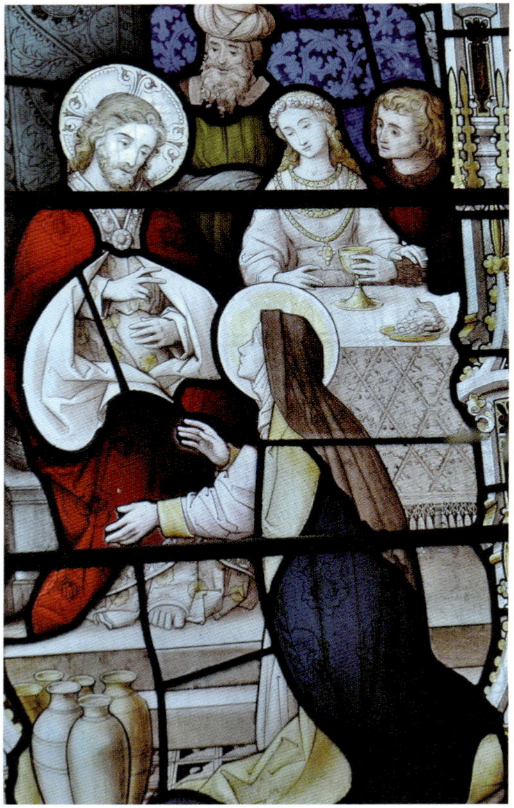

his power as the Son of God, Jesus quietly turns the water in the jars into a fine quality wine. So he saves the day in a hidden demonstration of practical compassion and care – but behind this miracle is a deeper meaning: Jesus has come to change the "water" of mere religion (endless rules and rituals) into the "new wine" of a relationship with the Living God – something to satisfy our spiritual thirst for ever.

[1] St John 1: 29

[2] St Matthew 3: 13 – 17

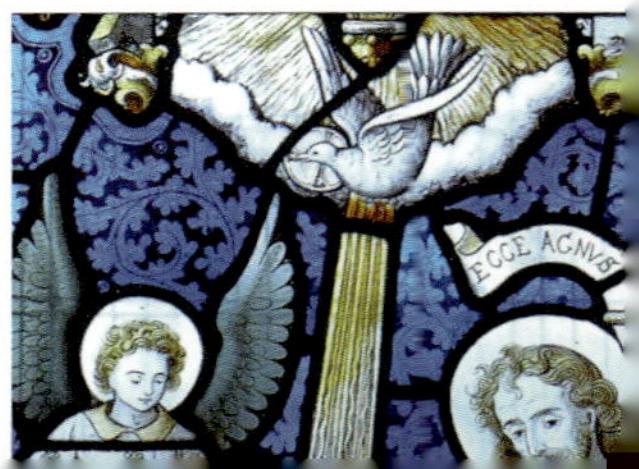

II

THE SANCTUARY EAST WINDOW

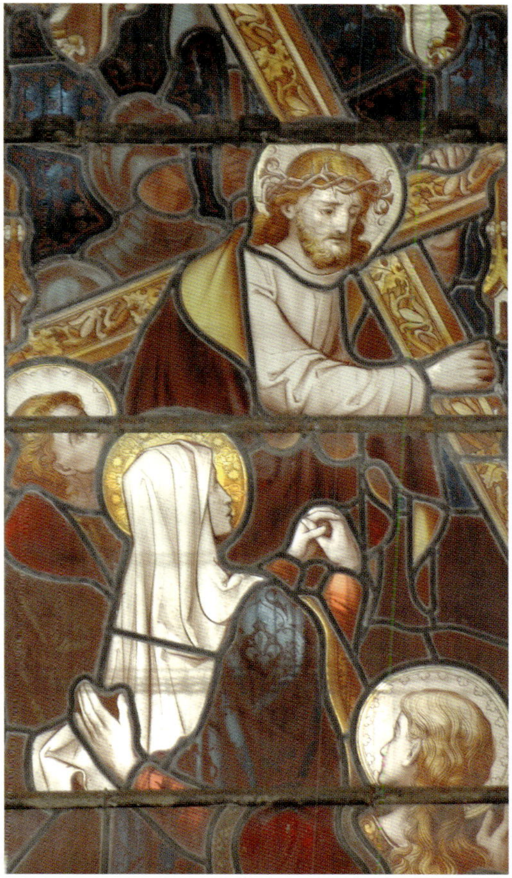

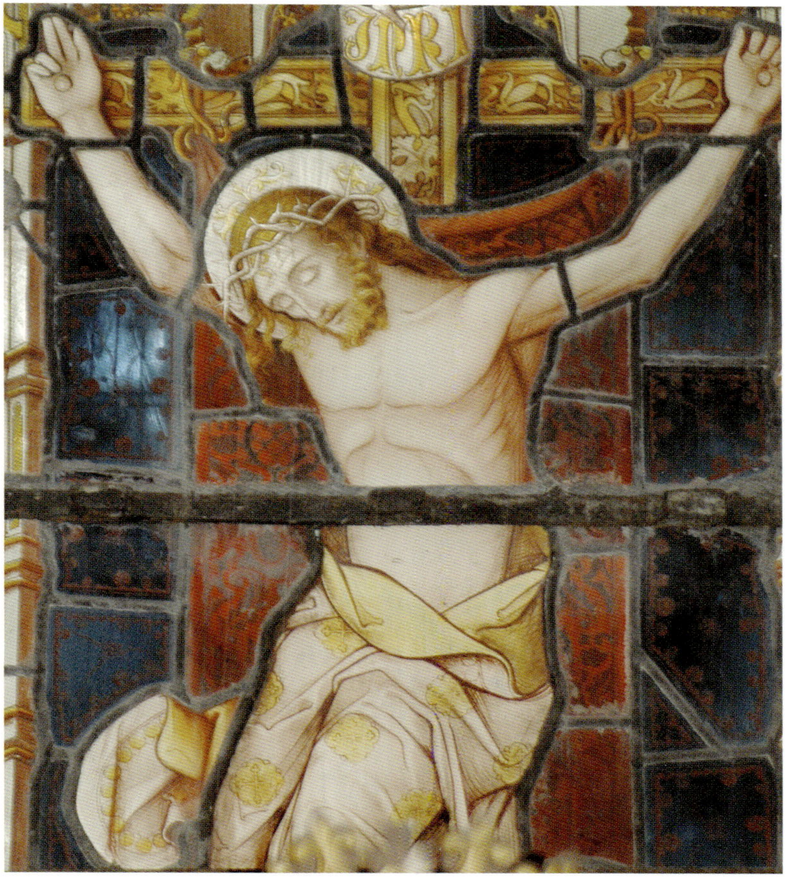

Part of this window is hidden by the early twentieth century wooden reredos, or altar piece, but the themes of the five largest lower panels are clear enough: From left to right, Jesus' birth; his carrying the cross to the place of execution; the crucifixion itself; his triumphant resurrection from the dead; and his ascension into heaven. Together these five present the essentials of the Christian Faith: that the man Jesus of Nazareth was none other than God come to earth in human form, to share in our sufferings, and then to rescue humankind from the bondage of sin and death by his atoning sacrifice and rising to new life.[1]

[1] 1 Corinthians 15: 1 - 4

12

THE SANCTUARY (South Side)

This window illustrates one of the most challenging parables Jesus ever told, sometimes called "The Sheep and the Goats". Found in St Matthew 25: 31 – 46, it describes the Last Judgement when all humanity will stand before Jesus Christ the King. Some (the sheep) will be rewarded with eternal life, whilst others (the goats) will be condemned to eternal punishment. The crucial question is: on what basis will the verdict be given? Jesus makes it clear that the sheep are those who have unwittingly served him by acts of mercy shown to the weak and vulnerable, whom he identifies as his "brothers". Hence the text in the upper part of the window: "In as much as ye have done it unto one of the least of my brethren, ye have done it unto me."[1] The four pictures opposite portray some examples of such service – feeding the hungry, visiting the prisoner, welcoming the stranger.

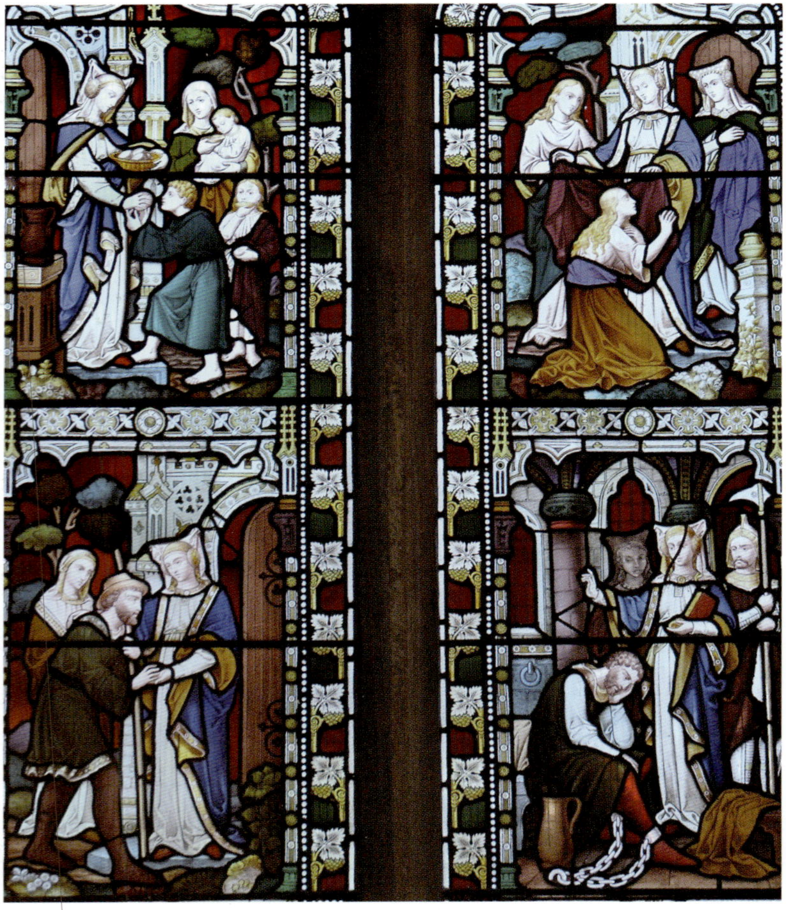

The goats are condemned for ignoring the needy, and therefore in fact ignoring Christ. The parable is a terrifying warning to the religious: just believing in God isn't nearly enough; genuine faith will always show itself in good deeds. "Faith without works is dead".[2]

[1] St Matthew 25: 40

[2] James 2: 17

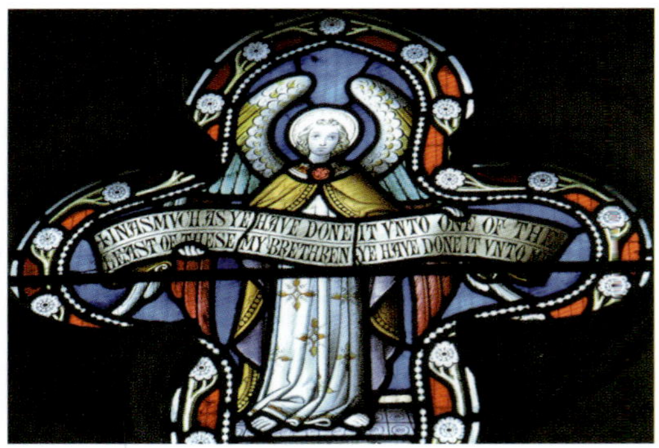

13

THE CHANCEL (South Side)

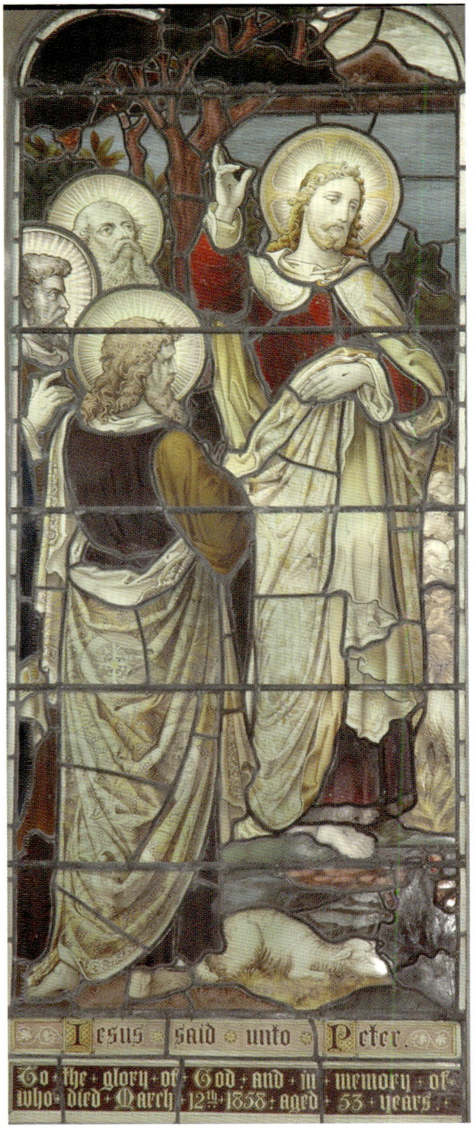

The risen Lord Jesus Christ in the left hand window is commissioning Peter, dressed in blue on the right, to "feed my sheep".[1] Peter is being instructed to lead the fledgling Christian Church, and in particular to nurture "the flock" by teaching them the great truths of the Faith. Peter understandably looks concerned: some weeks before he had let Jesus down badly by denying he was one of the disciples.[2] Was Jesus really giving him a second chance? Yes, God is always the God of the second chance – and the third, and the fourth! No failure of ours is irredeemable.

[1] St John 21: 15 – 17

[2] St Luke 22: 54 – 62

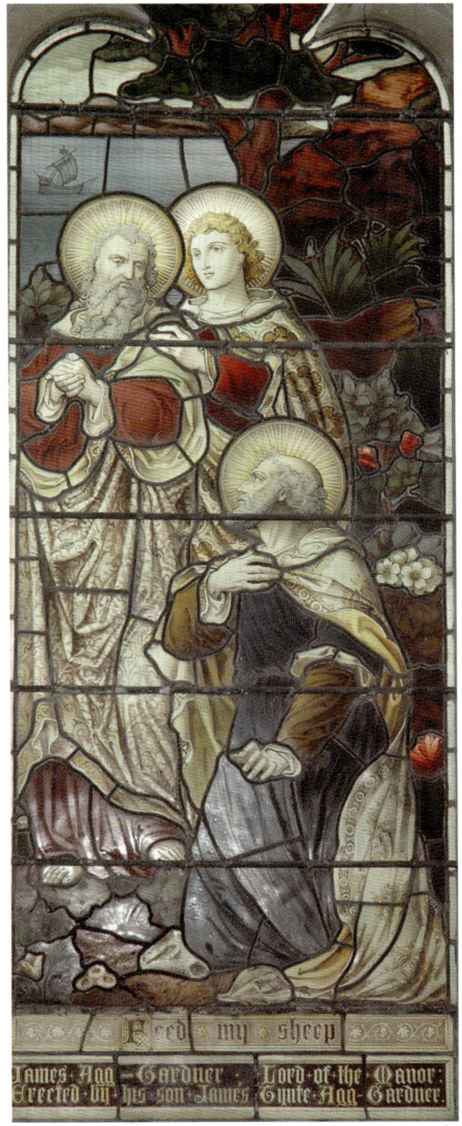

14

THE CHANCEL (South Side)

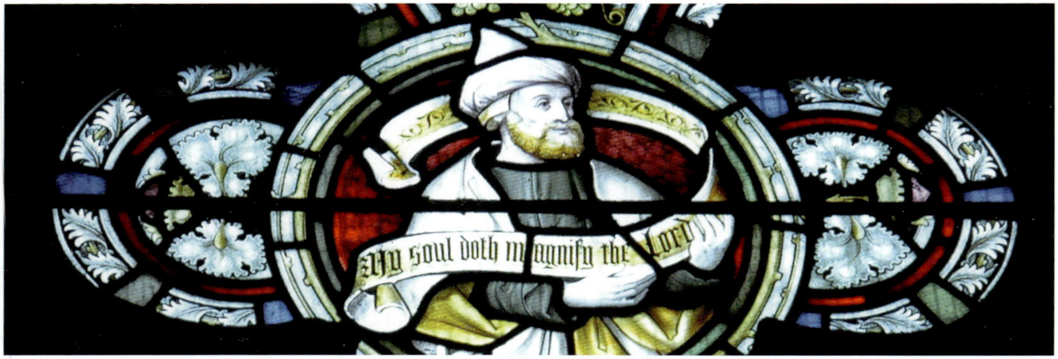

This window is about Christian worship. The text at the top - "My soul doth magnify the Lord" – is the opening line of Mary's song of praise, after learning she was to be the mother of the long expected Messiah;[1] but all believers will want to "magnify" the Lord – that is, to make him "bigger" in our thoughts and actions when life all around us conspires to "diminish" God in our hearts and minds.

One way we make God "bigger" is by regular worship, literally "worthship", or giving God what he is really worth. The two lower pictures give examples of Christian worship, perhaps depicting adoration, or confession.

God knows that we humans find it difficult to worship, or praise, him – so he has provided us with a wonderful worship "manual" or handbook: The Psalms! – one hundred and fifty of them, songs or hymns reflecting a whole range of human emotions, and therefore enabling us to approach God, whether we are feeling happy, sad, perplexed, full of faith, or doubt, or even in despair. Try reading some of the psalms out loud as your act of worship. If you're not sure where to start, Psalms 23, 95, 121, and 145 provide a good way in to this treasure store!

A question to reflect on: if it's a very long time since you last attended a church service, why do you think that is?

[1] St Luke 1: 46

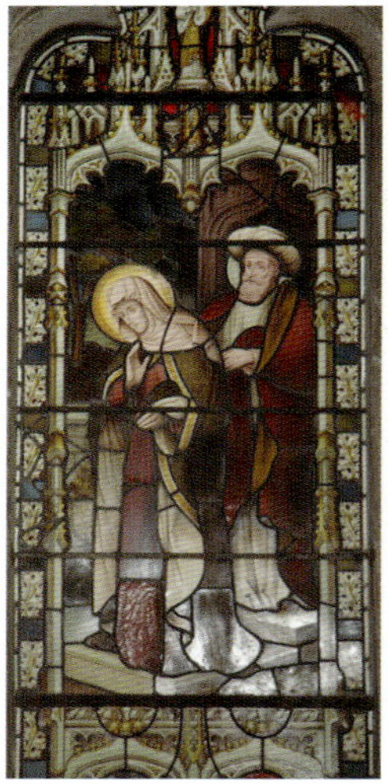

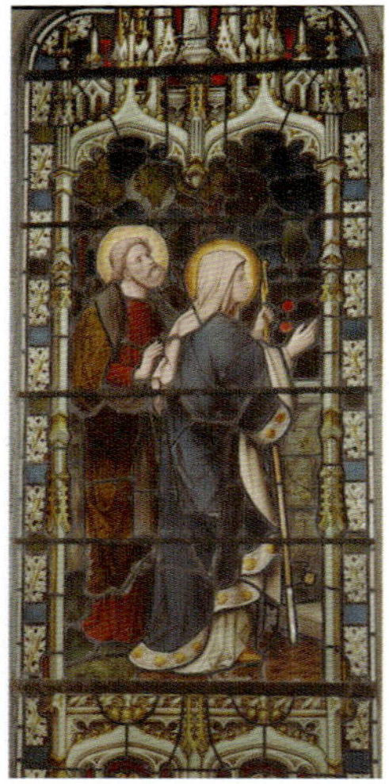

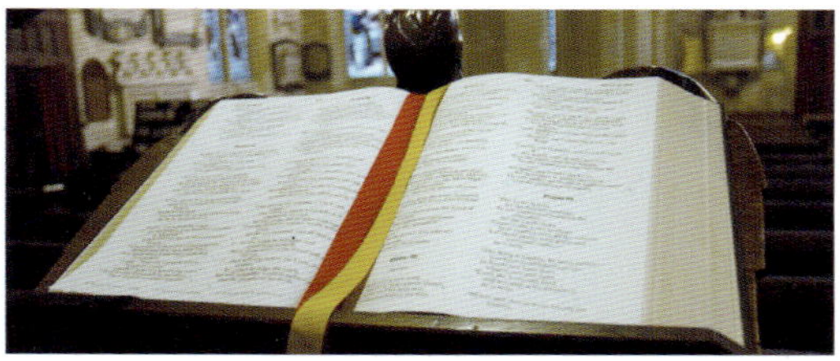

15 & 16

THE SOUTH TRANSEPT (East)

The three figures in the left hand window possibly represent the great Christian triad of Faith, Love, and Hope, three virtues or "graces" which are to characterize the lives of every professing Christian. Jesus was of course the greatest example of all three, and we need his Spirit deeply at work within us to show these attractive qualities.

The right hand window shows us three women all called Mary. Women feature prominently in the Bible accounts of Jesus' life (the four Gospels). Contrary to all the male prejudices of his time, Jesus befriended women and treated them with respect.

The centre window shows the Virgin Mary, the mother of Jesus. The Bible holds her up as an example of faith, purity, humility and obedience to the will of God.[1] Like so many of us, she struggled at first with believing in her son's unique identity and mission[2], but after Jesus' resurrection she takes an important place in the emerging Christian Church.[3]

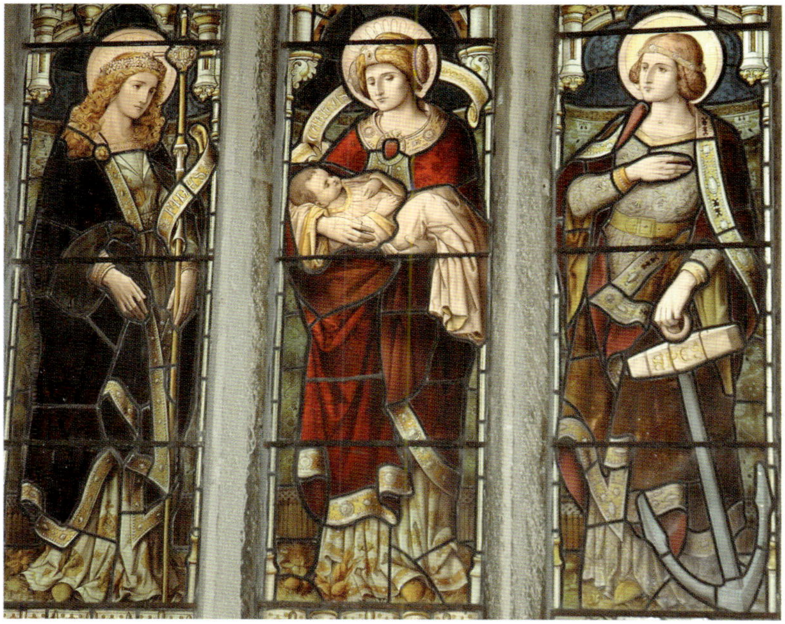

The figure in the left hand window is Mary Magdalene. She is shown holding a jar. The story in St Luke 7: 36 – 38 tells us that this contained some very valuable perfume, with which she anointed Jesus' feet, as her way of saying "Thank you" for all he had done for her. Later on, Mary Magdalene, visiting Jesus' burial place out of devotion to him, becomes one of the first witnesses of his resurrection, and has a special encounter with him near the site of his empty tomb![4]

According to the inscription in the flower-shaped window above, the third Mary is also called Cleopas. This identifies her with one of the two disciples who, on the first Easter Day, whilst walking from Jerusalem back to their home in Emmaus, are joined by a mystery traveller, whom they eventually invite to supper. This act of kindness does not go unrewarded: the stranger finally reveals himself as none other than Jesus risen from the dead![5] So this Mary Cleopas enjoys the priceless privilege of being one of the first witnesses to Jesus' pioneering conquest of death.

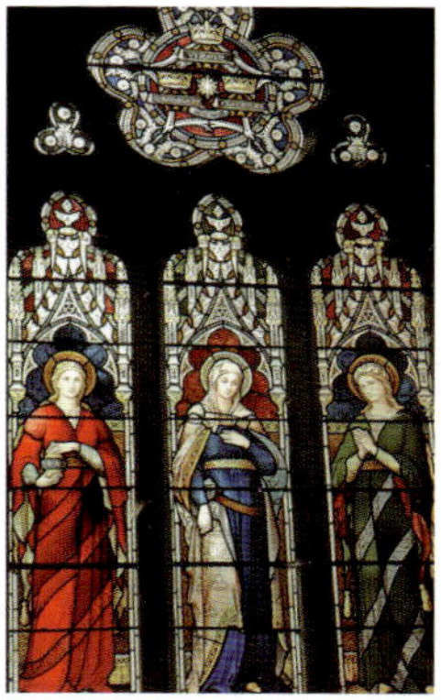

[1] St Luke 1: 28 – 30

[2] St Luke 2: 41 – 50

[3] Acts 1: 12 – 14

[4] John 20:1 – 18

[5] St Luke 24: 13 - 35

17

SOUTH TRANSEPT (South)

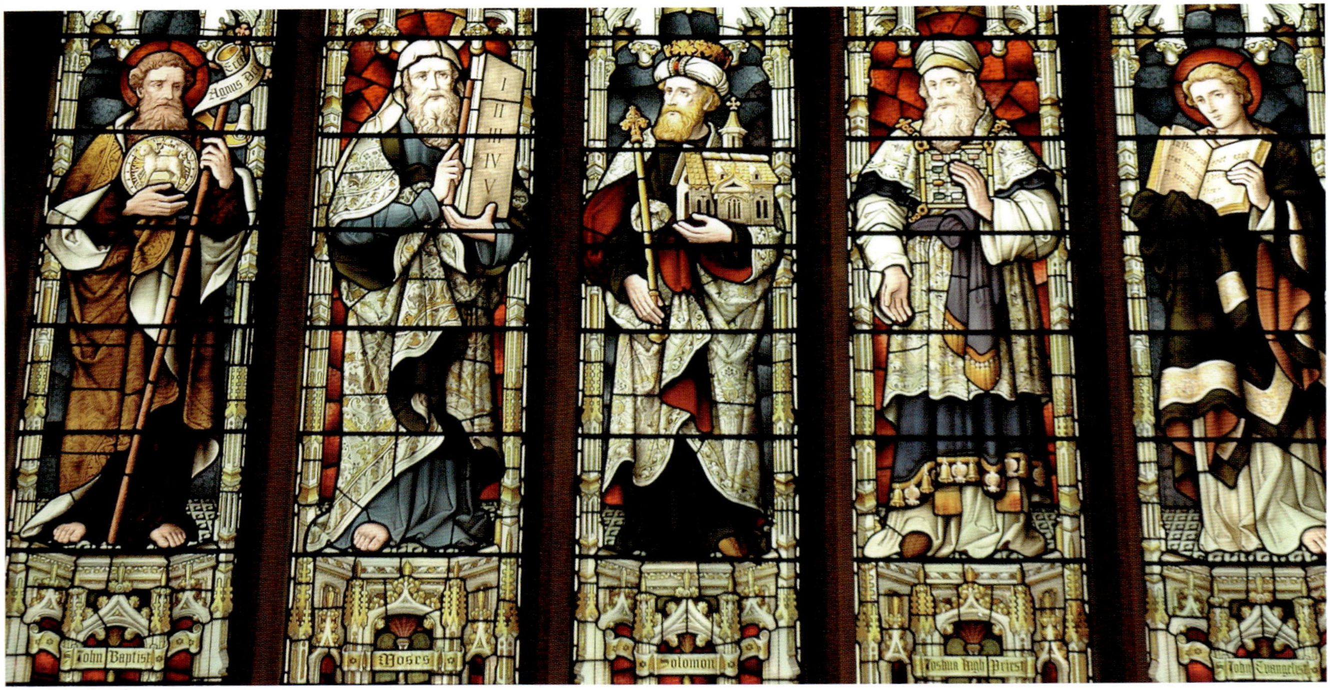

Five great heroes of faith stand before us here, reminding us that others have gone ahead of us, blazing a trail of obedience and commitment to God that we can follow. From left to right, they are: John the Baptist, Jesus' cousin and herald[1]; Moses, the great law-giver, seen holding the stone tablet containing the Ten Commandments[2]; King Solomon, who built the magnificent temple in Jerusalem[3]; Joshua the High Priest commissioned, despite his unworthiness for the task, to represent his people before God[4]; and St John the Evangelist (not to be confused with John the Baptist) who wrote five books of the New Testament, and was banished by the Roman authorities to the island of Patmos as a punishment for being a Christian.[5]

[1] St Luke 3: 1 – 18

[2] Exodus 20: 1 – 21

[3] 1 Kings 6

[4] Zechariah 3: 1 – 10

[5] Revelation 1: 9

18, 19 & 20

SOUTH AISLE

The middle window takes us to another of Jesus' well known stories, the Parable of the Talents.[1] A nobleman going on a journey has entrusted his money to three of his servants, on the clear understanding that they will invest it in some way, to earn interest for him. Two of the servants are diligent and successful, and on their master's return, receive a tremendous reward: a hearty "Well done…", and invitation to a closer friendship. A third servant, however, lazy and fearful, "buries his talent", and is condemned at the end. Jesus is clearly teaching that our lives are not our own – they are stewarded to us by God, to be used for his glory, and one day we will be called to account for what we have done with our years on earth.

[1] St Matthew 25: 14 – 30

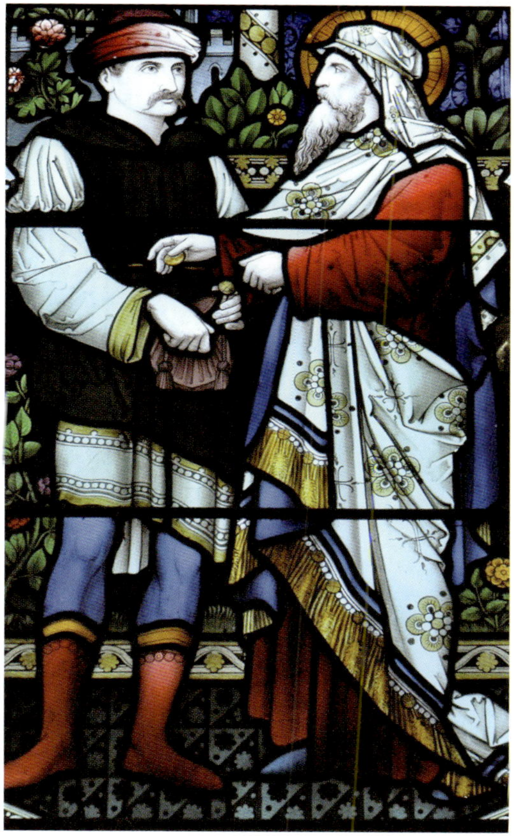

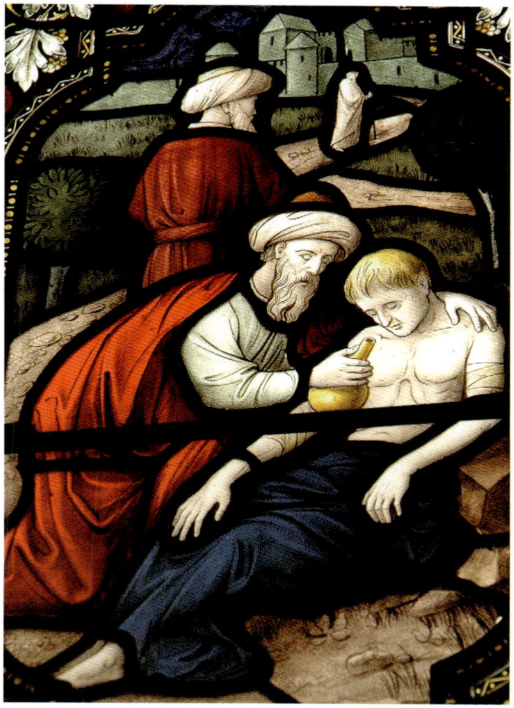

Look in the far right hand window at the ancient twisting steeply downhill Jericho road out of Jerusalem – you can travel it today, and it's still just as dramatic – which is the scene of Jesus' best known parable, the Good Samaritan, found in St Luke 10: 25 – 37. Given two thousand years of Christian moral teaching around this parable, many of us now completely miss the main thrust of the story! In our eyes, the Samaritan must be the "goodie", but to Jesus' first Jewish listeners, marinaded in hatred for the despised Samaritans, he will definitely be the "baddie". So as you read the parable, substitute for "But a Samaritan…" your own public enemy number one: a fat-cat banker, a suicide bomber, a convicted paedophile. Compassion and generosity can come from unexpected sources, teaches Jesus[1], as he pulls up short the self-righteous lawyer who questions him.

[1] St Luke 17: 18

18, 19 & 20

SOUTH AISLE (continued)

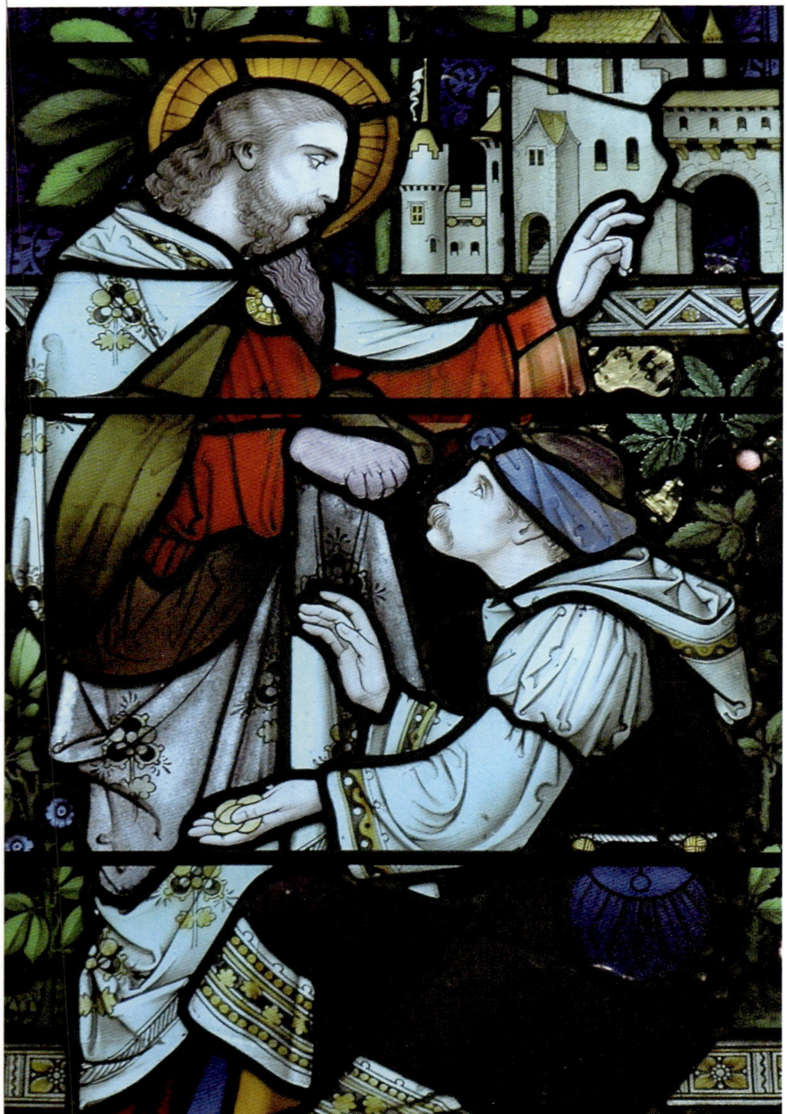

Notice in the picture the two religious types (the priest and the Levite) carefully avoiding the stricken traveller and hurrying on their way, no doubt full of the excuses instantly recognizable in ourselves: "I'm too busy to get involved…", "it's too risky to stop here…" Their refusal to help has immortalized an expression in our language: "To pass by on the other side." As the Bible teaches so forcefully, our sin is not necessarily wrong things we've done, but all the possible good we've neglected to do.

The Samaritan's costly act of mercy is of course a picture of Jesus' own rescue mission to earth: stooping down to our level, dressing our wounds, pouring on us the oil of his forgiveness and love, provision for our ongoing needs through the gift of his Spirit. Jesus doesn't tell us whether the traveller's rescue by someone supposed to be his enemy changed his life in any way (that would be narrative overload) – but the question remains: How does this age-old tale affect our everyday lives now? Who is my neighbour?

21

SOUTH AISLE (Beyond the South Porch)

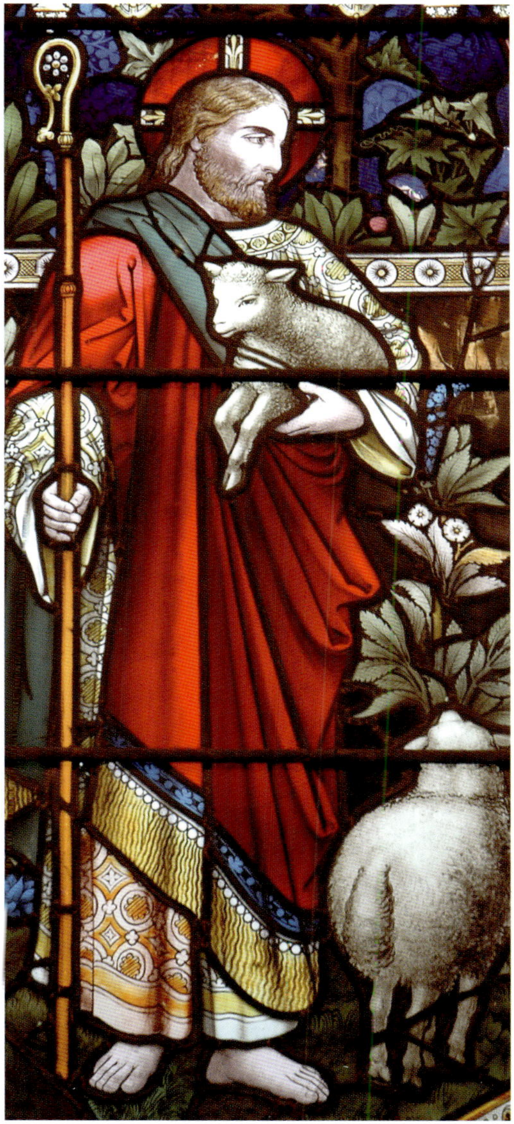

Two pictures highlight the love and compassion of Jesus. The first depicts him as "The Good Shepherd", a title he ascribed to himself,[1] and in the Jewish culture of his time, a clear claim to being divine.[2] Just as any good shepherd knows his flock intimately, so Jesus knows each one of his followers, and cares for them, even to the extent of giving his life for them.The Bible is unflattering in its view of people: we are all like sheep – prone to "go astray" and "get lost".[3] We need the Good Shepherd to search for us, and bring us home to the safety of the "fold" where we belong.[4]

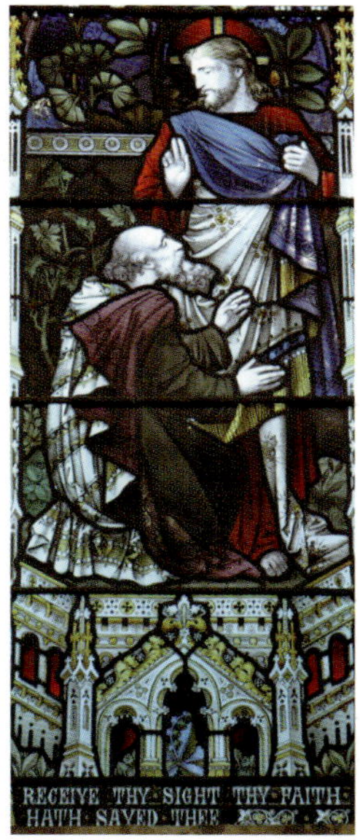

Typical of his pastoral compassion was Jesus' concern for the disabled, especially the blind and the lame. The second window shows Jesus miraculously restoring eyesight to a blind beggar. Bartimaeus, as he is called in one of the gospels, had persistently cried out to him for mercy, a clear sign to Jesus of genuine faith.[5] It's not the amount of faith we have that counts, it's the direction in which it's looking; a heartfelt cry to God for mercy is a plea he will not ignore.

As with many of Jesus' healing miracles, the physical cure is a sign of something deeper Jesus wants to do. He once described himself as "The Light of the World", the One who can "open our eyes" to vital spiritual truths, about God, ourselves, life, death and the world.[6]

[1] St John 10: 11 – 15

[2] Psalm 23: 1

[3] Isaiah 53: 6

[4] 1 Peter 2: 25

[5] St Luke 18: 35 – 43

[6] St John 8: 12

22

THE LAST SUPPER WINDOW

The Gospels tell us that on the Thursday night before he died, Jesus celebrated the Jewish Feast of the Passover with his twelve special friends.[1] This annual festival recalled the dramatic way God rescued his people from slavery in Egypt many centuries before.[2] Jesus, however, gives the meal a completely new meaning for his followers: it will become a memorial celebration of the dramatic way God has rescued all humankind from a different sort of slavery – to selfishness and sin. This was to be achieved by Jesus' sacrificial death on the cross, the very next day (Good Friday)!

Notice in the central panel the bread and cup of wine being blessed by Jesus. He told his friends that the broken bread was to act as a powerful symbol of his own body, soon to be broken by crucifixion; and the wine would represent his blood shed.[3]

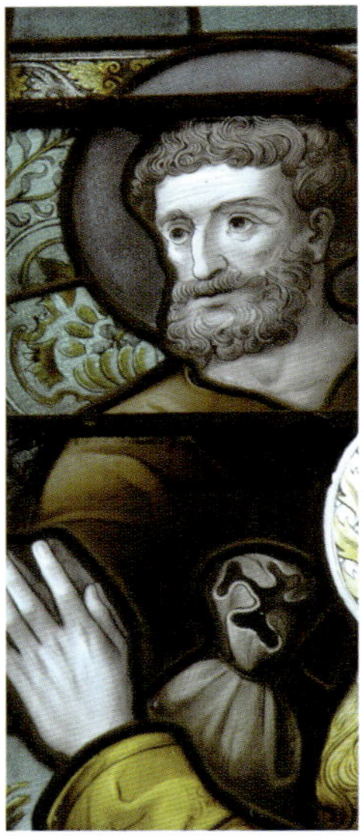

[1] St Mark 14: 1 – 25

[2] Exodus 12: 1 – 30

[3] St Matthew 26: 26 – 28

For the last two thousand years, Christians have gratefully remembered the death of Jesus on their behalf by holding services where everyone present eats a piece of bread and takes a sip of wine. These services are called "Holy Communion" or "The Eucharist" or "The Lord's Supper", and can be a vital encouragement to the faith and commitment of those taking part.

Of course, taking Holy Communion doesn't guarantee closeness to God. Can you see the disciple with the brown halo in the far right panel? This is probably Judas Iscariot, who was already scheming with Jesus' enemies to betray him for money, and who would later that night slip away from the feast to meet with them. The key question is: Where do our loyalties lie? Whose side are we really on?

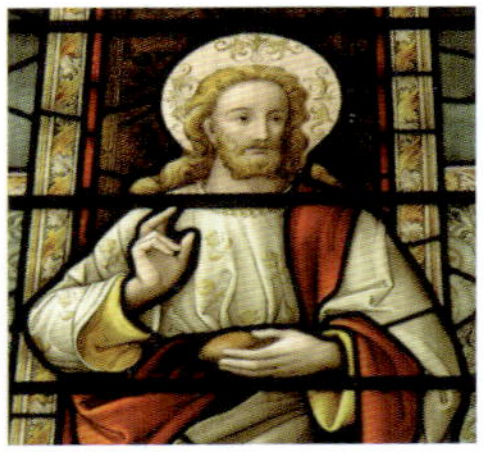

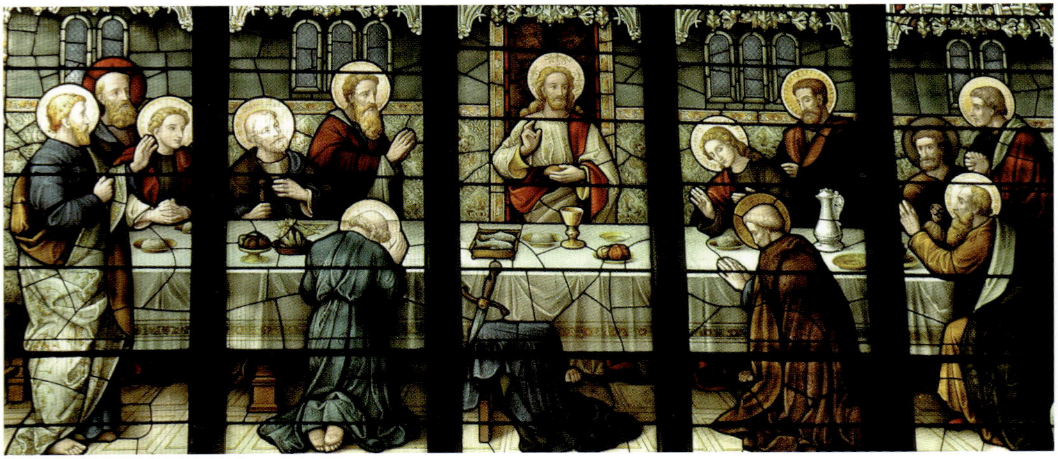

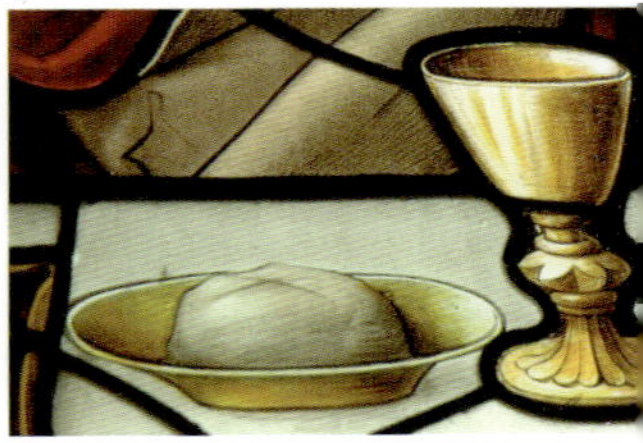

23

THE CENTRAL WEST WINDOW

The three central panes depict three scenes from the life of Christ, beginning with his birth in the centre. We see his mother, the Virgin Mary, looking at the infant Jesus, with his earthly father, Joseph, standing behind her. The Bible is clear that the story is a historical event, set in a real place – Bethlehem – during the reign of a well known king, Herod the Great.[1] The inscription beneath tells us one of the very special names given to this unique baby: "Emmanuel", which means "God with us".[2] This brings us to the very heart of Christianity – the good news that God cared so much about us that he came to earth as a baby, just like each one of us – he stepped into our shoes, and so can understand and help us in life's struggles.

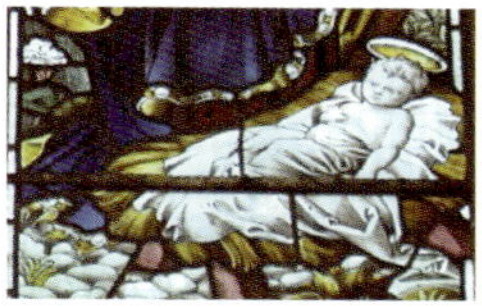

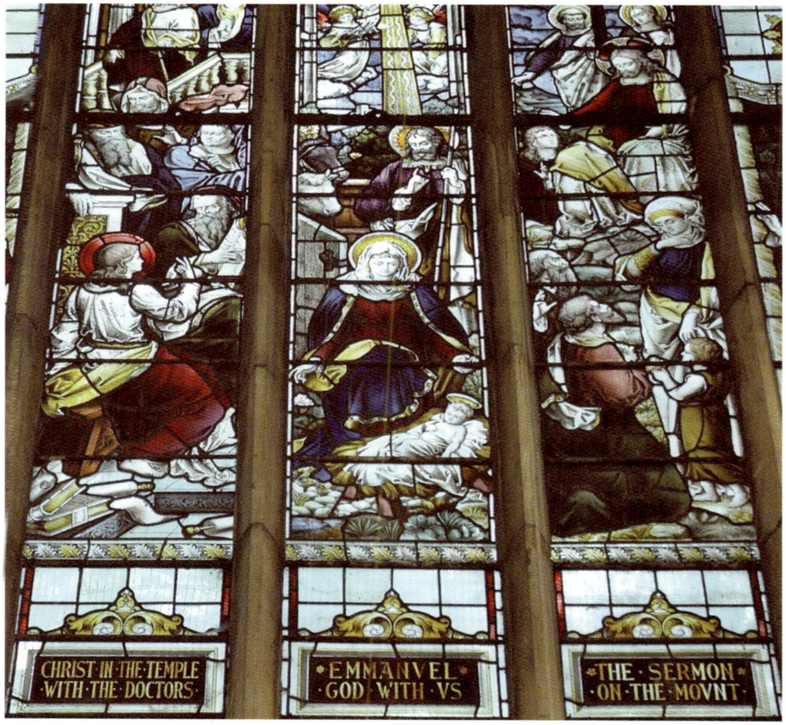

The window on the left reveals an incident from Jesus' childhood which is told in St Luke 2: 41 – 52. At the age of twelve, Jesus' parents took him to Jerusalem for the annual Passover Feast. When they went home, Jesus stayed behind in Jerusalem, discussing religion with the teachers ("the doctors") in the temple. They were amazed at his understanding at such an early age: Jesus was already becoming aware of his unique identity and special God-given mission.

The right hand window shows Jesus teaching his followers through what is often called "The Sermon on the Mount". You can read the sermon in St Matthew chapters 5–7. Many people rather glibly claim to live their lives according to all the rules set out in the sermon, but they don't – nobody does! They set a standard of perfection out of reach for most of us. So why did Jesus teach it? One reason was to show us what true purity of life is really like, and so to expose our own need of God's forgiveness and inner cleansing, before we attempt to follow his ways.

[1] St Matthew 2: 1

[2] St Matthew 1: 18 – 23

24

THE ASCENSION WEST WINDOW

This large window depicts the event in the Bible that Christians call Jesus' Ascension. It took place in Jerusalem, on the Mount of Olives (which you can visit today), as Jesus said a final "Good-bye" to his friends, and returned to his Father God in the eternal world (Heaven). You can read the story in St Luke 24: 50 – 51, and Acts 1: 9 – 11. The text at the bottom of the window is taken from The Apostles' Creed, an early summary of the Church's beliefs about Jesus, and it sums up the vital significance of Jesus' ascension: it was a clear sign to his followers that he would no longer remain on earth, rather, he was taking his deserved place "at God's right hand". Obviously we don't take this phrase literally – it's a symbolic way of saying that Jesus has been given the position of supreme authority in the universe, he is the King – and his ascension was his public coronation.

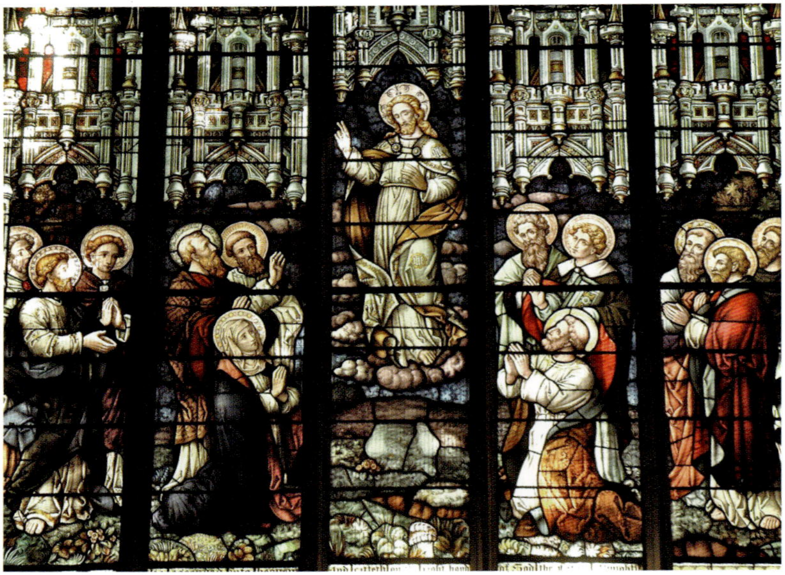

The Bible story tells us that after Jesus had been hidden by a cloud, two supernatural messengers promised the disciples that one day Jesus would return in glory. This is an event (sometimes called the Second Coming) that every Christian eagerly awaits and tries to prepare for. It's a fitting thought for the end of our tour of the windows: If Jesus were to return in majestic splendour tonight, would I be able to welcome him gladly, or would I be embarrassed by my lack of faith and commitment?

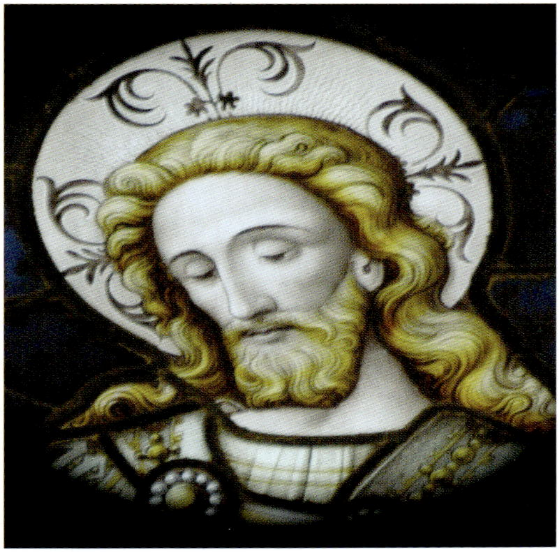

1

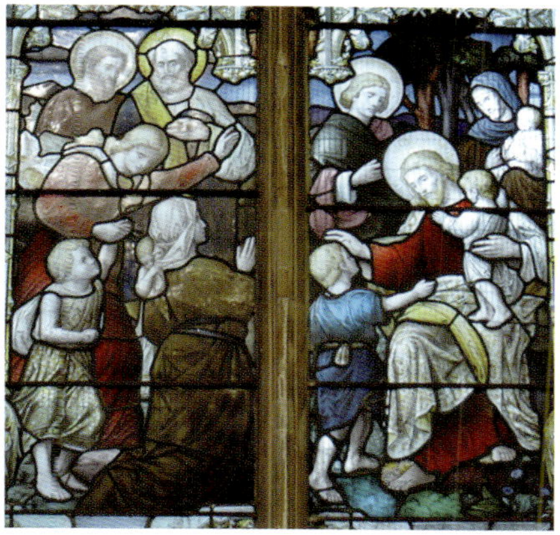

2, 3 & 4

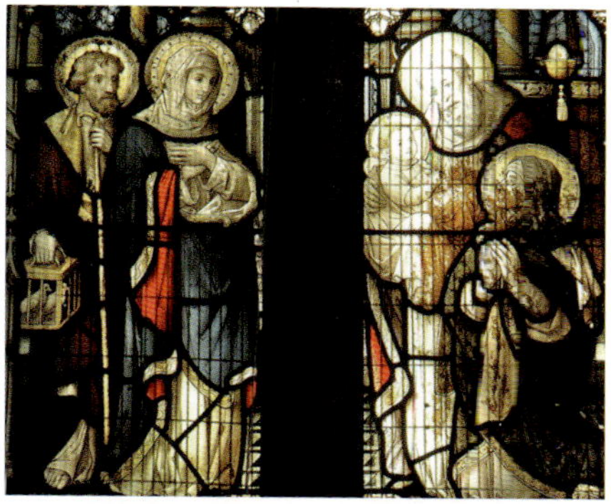

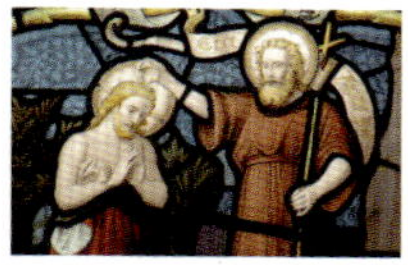

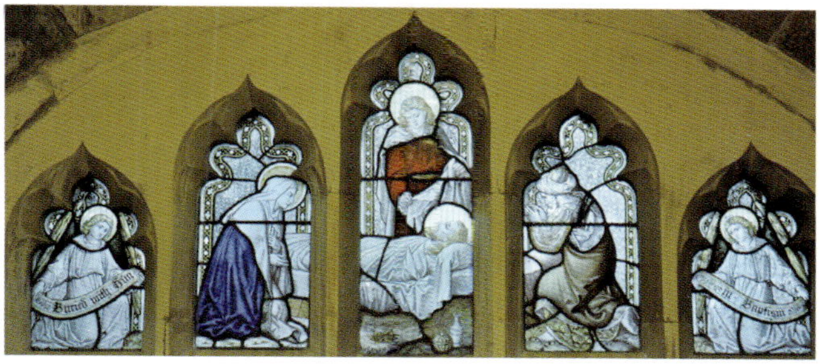

5 & 6

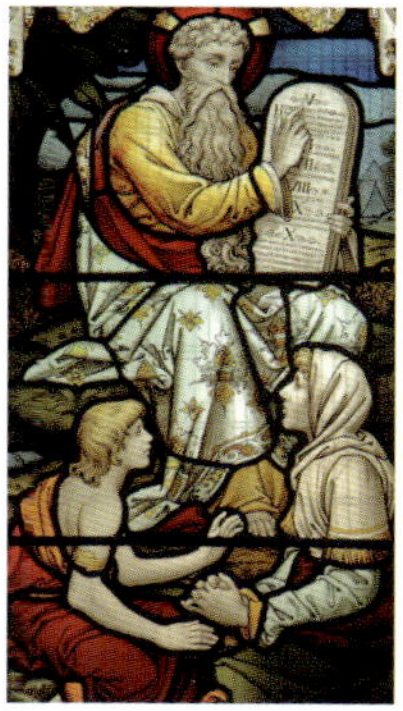

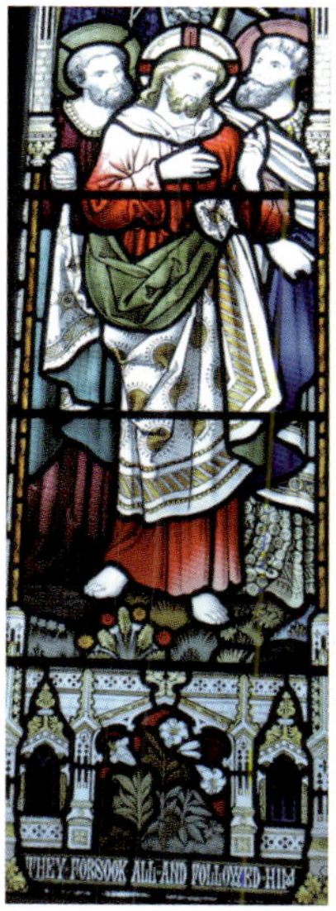
THEY FORSOOK ALL AND FOLLOWED HIM

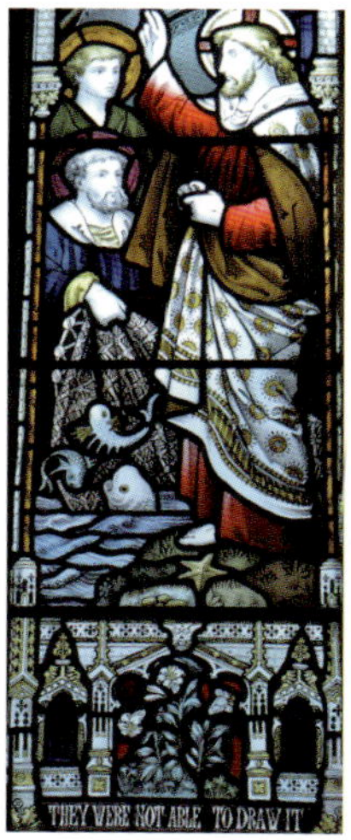
THEY WERE NOT ABLE TO DRAW IT

7

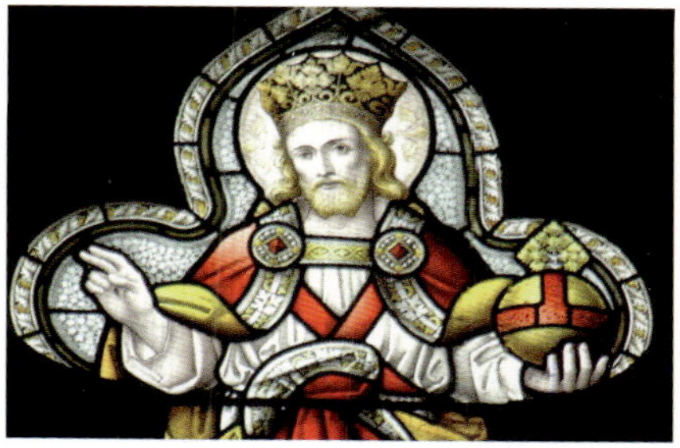

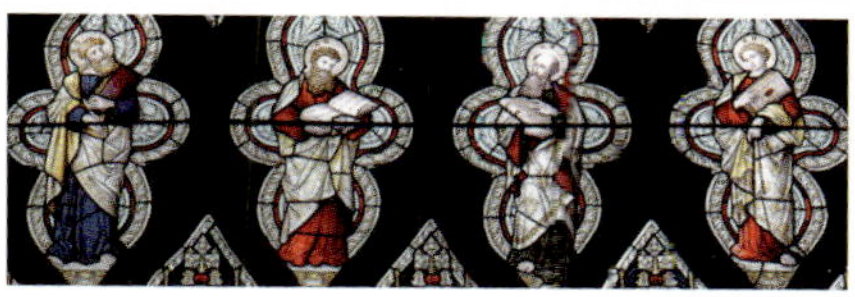

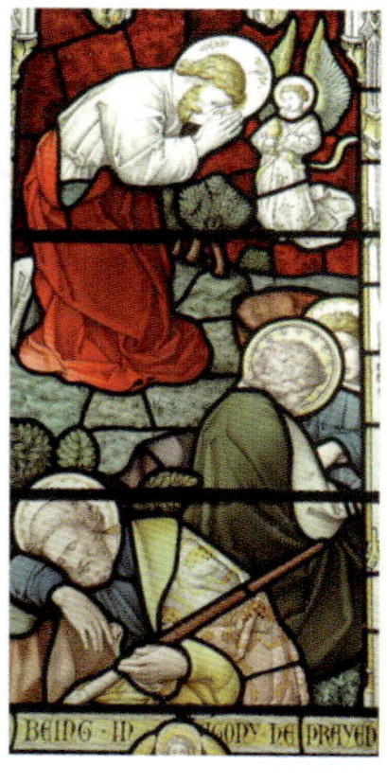

8

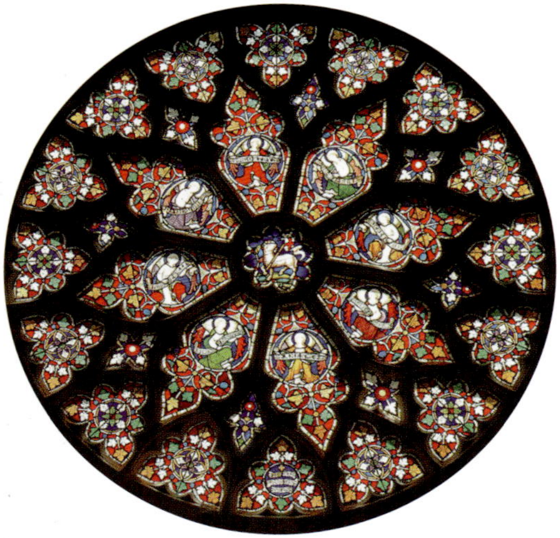

9

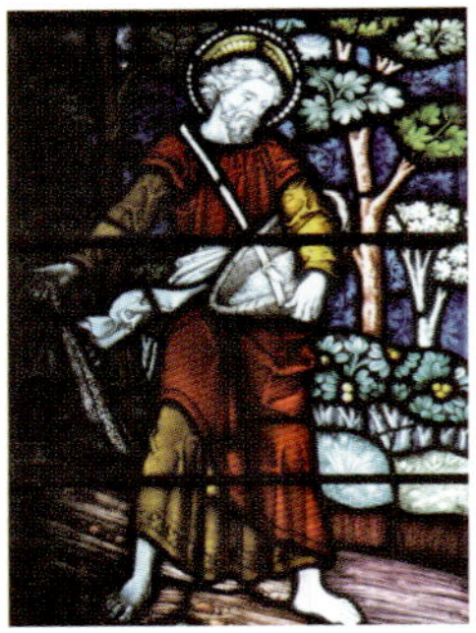

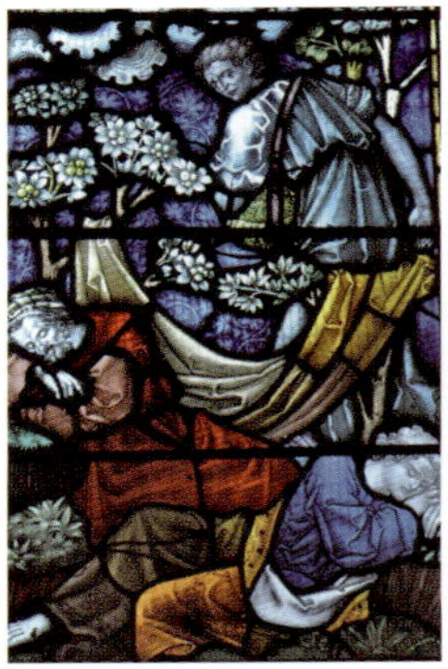

10

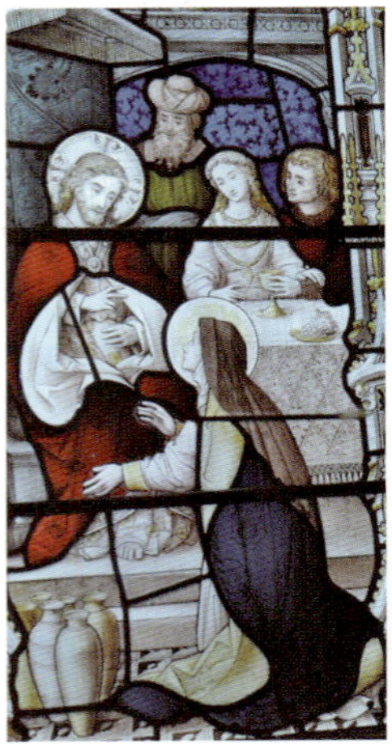

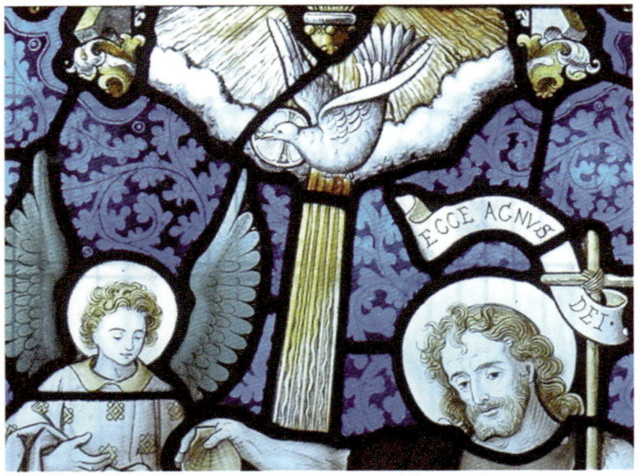

11

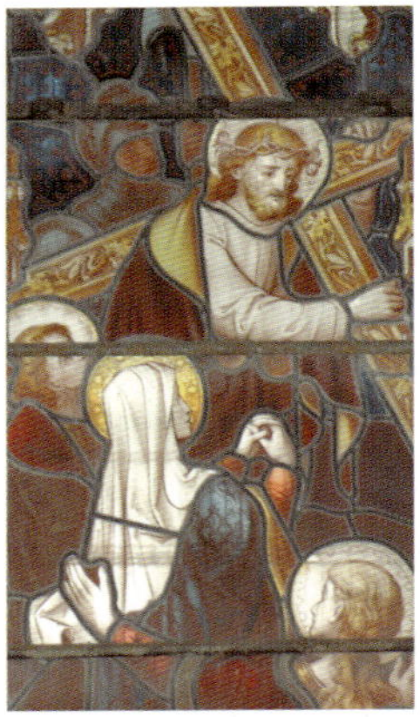

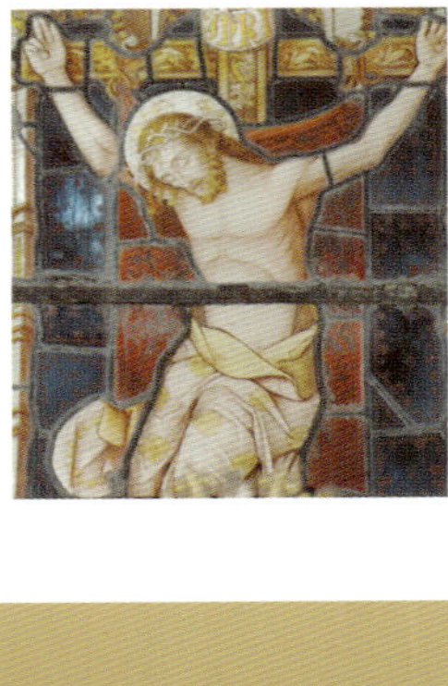

12

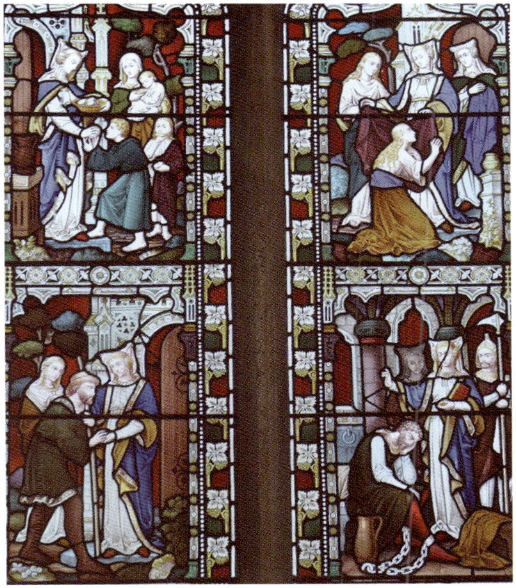

13

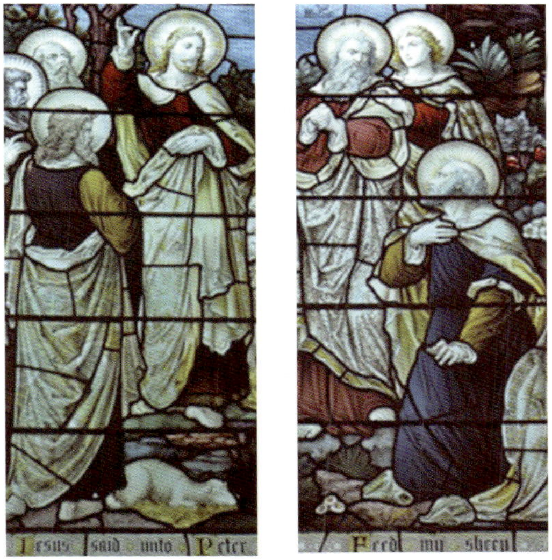

14

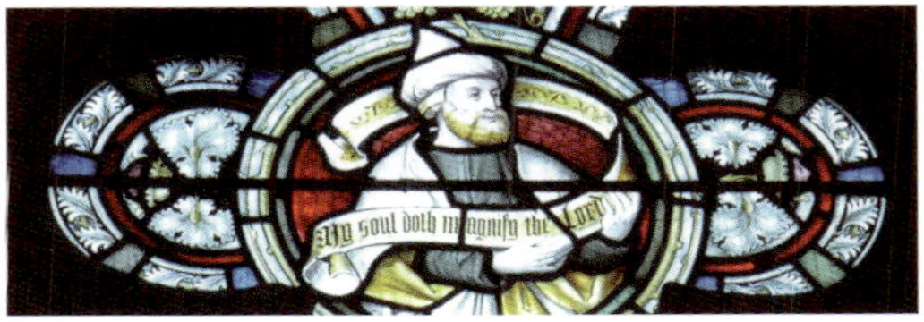

15 & 16

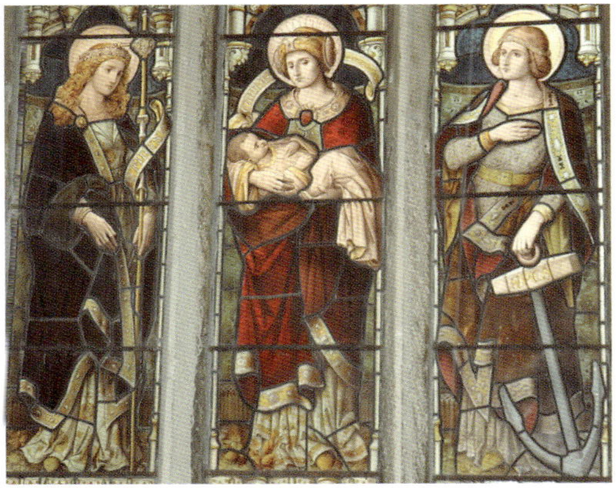

17

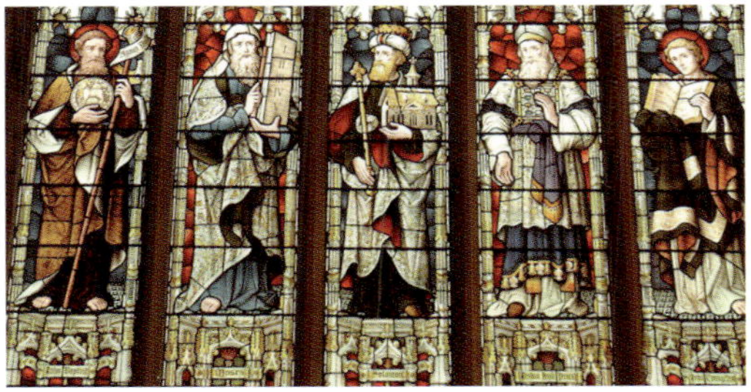

18, 19 & 20

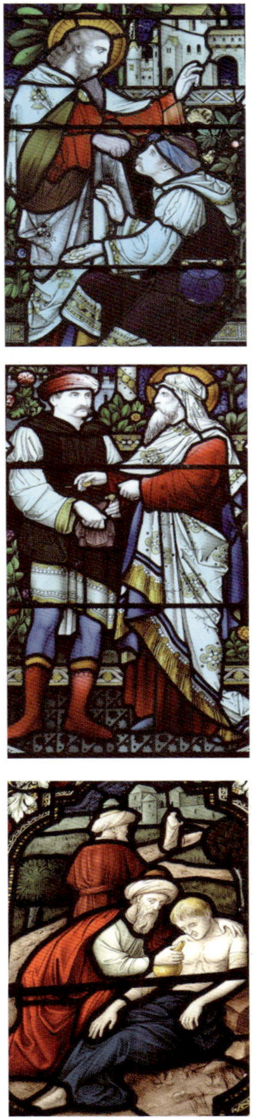

21

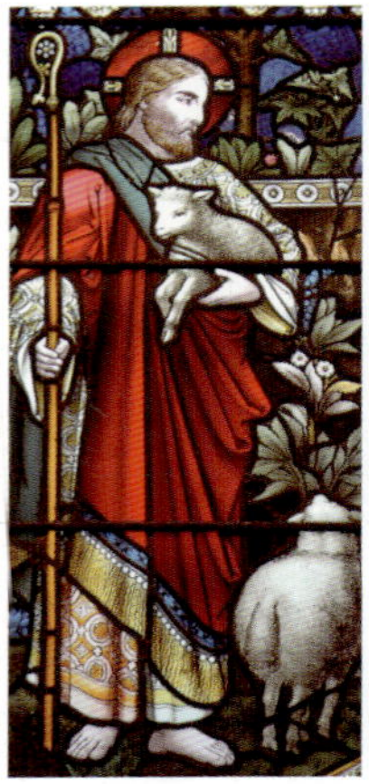

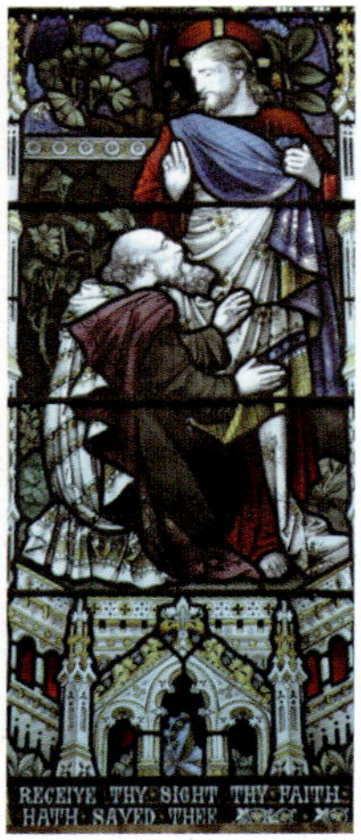
RECEIVE THY SIGHT THY FAITH
HATH SAVED THEE

22

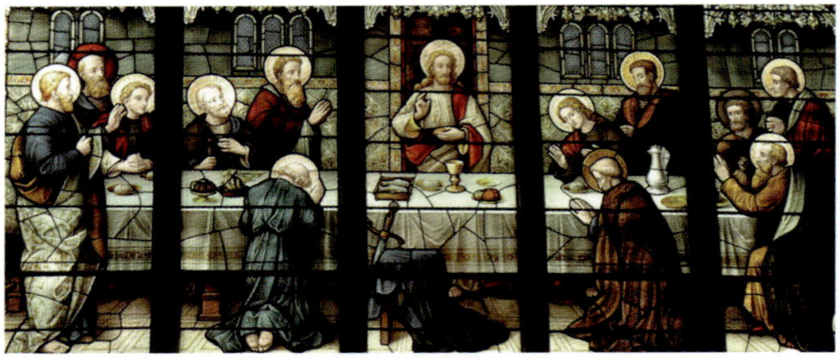

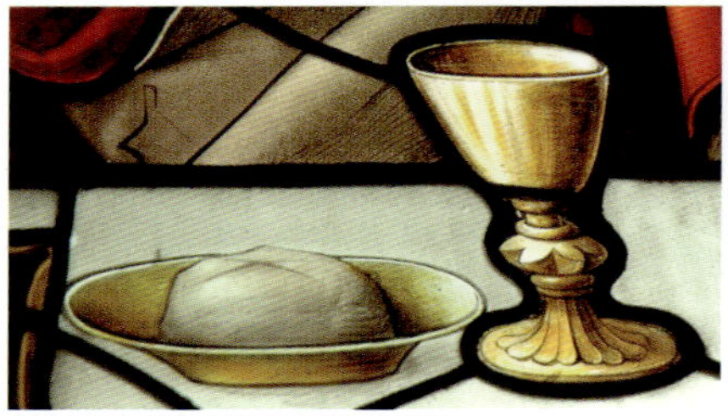

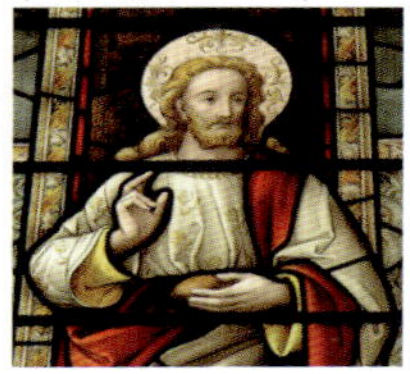

23

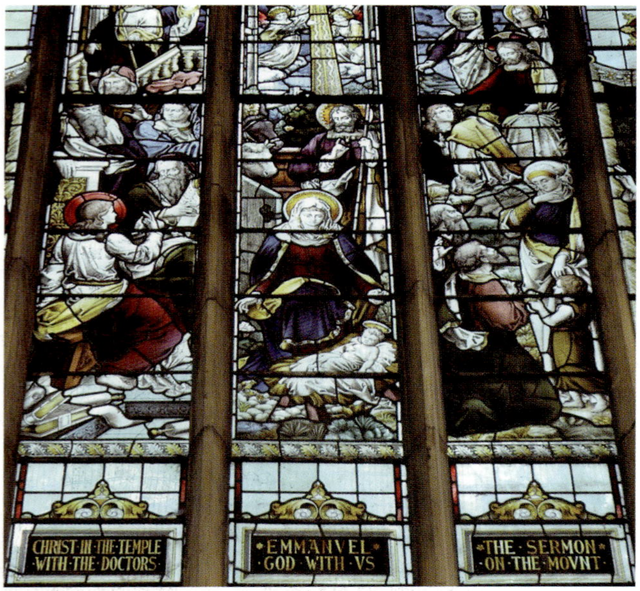
CHRIST·IN·THE·TEMPLE
·WITH·THE·DOCTORS·
·EMMANVEL·
·GOD·WITH·VS·
·THE·SERMON·
·ON·THE·MOVNT·

24

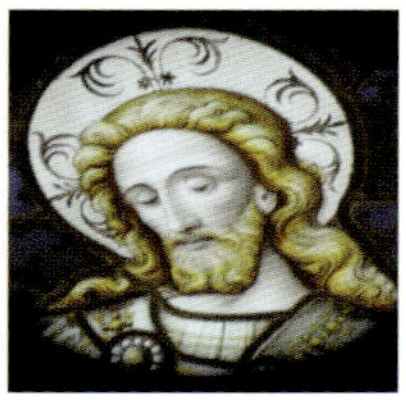

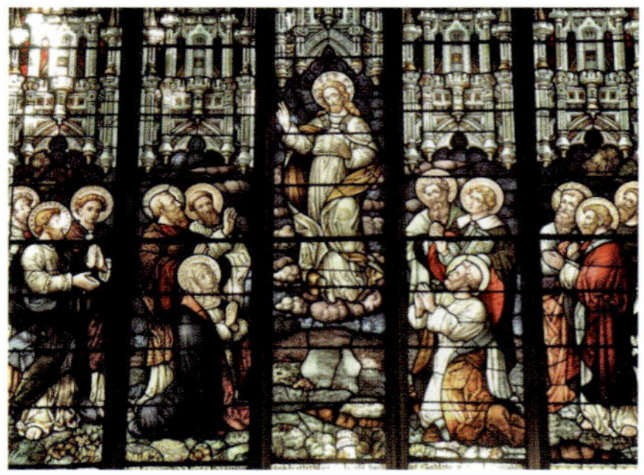